Book Four

D1604719

Program Authors

**Linda Ward Beech • James Beers • Jo Ann Dauzat
Sam V. Dauzat • Tara McCarthy**

Program Consultants

Myra K. Baum
Office of Adult and
   Continuing Education
Brooklyn, New York

Francis J. Feltman, Jr.
Racine Youth Offender
   Correctional Facility
Racine, Wisconsin

Mary Ann Guilliams
Gary Job Corps
San Marcos, Texas

Julie Jacobs
Inmate Literacy Project
Santa Clara County Library
Milpitas, California

Maxine L. McCormick
Workforce Education
Orange County Public Schools
Orlando, Florida

Sandra S. Owens
Laurens County Literacy Council
Laurens, South Carolina

STECK-VAUGHN
ELEMENTARY · SECONDARY · ADULT · LIBRARY

A Harcourt Company

www.steck-vaughn.com

Acknowledgments

Staff Credits

Executive Editor: Ellen Northcutt

Senior Editor: Donna Townsend

Associate Design Director: Joyce Spicer

Supervising Designer: Pamela Heaney

Designer: Jessica Bristow

Production Coordinator: Rebecca Gonzales

Electronic Production Artist: Julia Miracle-Hagaman

Senior Technical Advisor: Alan Klemp

Electronic Production Specialist: Dina Bahan

Photography Credits

Cover (women in kitchen) Park Street; (father & son) Christine Galida; (party) Ken Lax; (Ben Knighthorse) © Dave Bartruff/CORBIS; p.2 © AP/Wide World Photos; p.10 (l) © Dave Bartruff/CORBIS; p.10 ® © Rotolo/Liaison Agency; p.10 © Corbis; pp.18, 26 Park Street; pp.34, 42 Christine Galida; pp.50, 58 Ken Walker; pp.66, 76 Park Street; pp.82, 91 Ken Lax; p.98 Jeff Gritchen; pp.118-119 © PhotoDisc; p.106 Jeff Gritchen.

Literary Credits

"It Couldn't Be Done," from *The Collected Verse of Edgar A. Guest*. Copyright © 1934 by Contemporary Books, Inc. Reprinted by permission of Contemporary Books, Inc.

ISBN 0-7398-2842-8

Printed in the United States of America

Contents

To the Learner

In this book, you will read interesting stories and develop your reading skills. The book has seven units. Each unit has a story about a different topic. As you read the stories, you will review words you already know and learn new words. You will also learn and practice a writing skill, a reading comprehension skill, and a life skill. Then you will have a review to check the skills you have learned in the unit before you move on to the next unit.

After you have completed all seven units, there is a Final Review that gives you a chance to check all the skills you have learned in the book.

In the At Your Leisure section at the end of the book, you will have a chance to read just for fun. This section has a poem and another reading selection for you to enjoy.

Have a good time using this book. It is written for you!

Instructor's Notes: Read this page to students. Discuss having students keep a notebook or journal of words and original sentences they write. Refer to the *Reading for Today Instructor's Guide* for lesson plans, optional teaching activities, and a discussion of how to use the Learner Placement Form on the inside back cover of this book.

Unit 1 Living an Active Life

Discussion

Remember

Look at the picture. What work do you think this man does?

Predict

Look at the picture and the story title. What do you think the story is about?

One Man, Many Jobs:
Ben Nighthorse Campbell

Ben Nighthorse Campbell is a man with many jobs. Some of the time, he's working on his land. Some of the time he's in the city doing the job he was picked to do, taking action on problems people have. When he has time, he works on the job that he learned as a child.

The story continues.

Instructor's Notes: Read the discussion questions with students. Discuss the story title and the situation in the picture. Explain that this story is based on the life of a real person. Read Campbell's full name and have students repeat it. Explain that Campbell is from the state of Colorado. Then have students read silently. Have them underline words they don't recognize. Review the underlined words.

3

Unit 1

Review Words

A. Check the words you know.

☐ **1.** still   ☐ **2.** because   ☐ **3.** hold

☐ **4.** many   ☐ **5.** working   ☐ **6.** people

☐ **7.** together   ☐ **8.** different   ☐ **9.** does

☐ **10.** action   ☐ **11.** child   ☐ **12.** more

B. Read and write the sentences. Circle the review words.

1. Ben Nighthorse Campbell takes action in many different ways.

_____

2. Campbell still does a job he learned as a child.

_____

3. He is good at working together with different people.

_____

4. Campbell holds down more than one job because he can do many things well.

_____

C. Write the word that means the opposite of the underlined word.

1. The opposite of <u>same</u> is _____ .

2. The opposite of <u>one</u> is _____ .

3. The opposite of <u>playing</u> is _____ .

Instructor's Notes: Read each set of directions with students. For A, have students read the words aloud and then check known words. Have students practice any unknown words in a notebook or journal. For C, explain that words that are opposite are also called *antonyms*.

Sight Words

law ● been ● here
American Indian

A. Read the words above. Then read the sentence.

Laws have **been** helping **American Indians here** in the United States.

B. Underline the sight words in sentences 1–5.

1. Ben Nighthorse Campbell is an American Indian.

2. He has been of help to people with problems.

3. Campbell works to make bills into laws.

4. American Indians want action on these laws.

5. There have been problems about the water rights of different groups here.

C. Write the word that best completes each sentence.

American Indians   laws   here   been

1. Campbell's home is _____ in the United States.

2. He works on water rights for _____ .

3. He has _____ a key player in taking action.

4. How does Campbell help make _____ ?

D. Read the sentences. Underline the sight words.

The land and water in the United States are different from when American Indians lived on the land. People came to the United States to make homes here and took a lot of the land. They have used up or hurt the water in some way. Campbell has been working to make laws that fix these problems.

Instructor's Notes: Read each set of directions with students. For A, read each sight word aloud. Have students repeat. Discuss the use of the terms *American Indian* and *Native American.* Explain that Senator Campbell works to protect natural resources and public lands in Colorado.

Sight Words

elected ● senator
horse ● ranch

A. Read the words above. Then read the sentences.

Campbell was **elected senator** in the fall of 1992. Sometimes he has to put the work on his **horse ranch** on hold.

B. Underline the sight words in sentences 1–3.

1. People elected Campbell because he is a man of action.

2. In the United States senators are elected to help make laws.

3. Senator Campbell owns and runs a horse ranch as well.

C. Write the word that best completes each sentence.

horses   senator   ranch   elected

1. Senators are _____ by the people.

2. Being a _____ is a big job.

3. One of Campbell's many loves is working on his

_____ .

4. He works with quarter _____ on his ranch.

D. Read the sentences. Underline the sight words.

At his ranch, Senator Campbell can ride horses and work with his ranch hands. He doesn't have the time for his ranch that he used to, but he gets there when he can. He gives his job as senator his all because he was elected by the people.

Instructor's Notes: Read each set of directions with students. For A, read each sight word aloud. Have students repeat. Explain that Colorado is Campbell's home state and where his ranch is located. As a senator, he works in Washington, D.C.

6

Unit 1

Sight Words   put ● silver   jewelry ● again

A. Read the words above. Then read the sentence.

With all the work Campbell has to **put** in as a senator and a rancher, he will have to find time to make **silver jewelry again**.

B. Underline the sight words in sentences 1–4.

1. Campbell learned how to make jewelry when he was a child.

2. Campbell's teacher in jewelry making was his father.

3. He sometimes puts stones in his silver jewelry.

4. People who like his work come to him for jewelry again.

C. Write the word that best completes each sentence.

     jewelry   silver   again   puts

1. You can see the time Campbell _____ into his work.

2. The _____ jewelry is sold in stores.

3. People look at it _____ and again.

4. Campbell likes to put horses on his _____ .

D. Read the sentences. Underline the sight words.

Will Campbell find time to make more silver jewelry? He says he won't give up doing work he likes this well. He works on the silver jewelry at night. That way he can go to his job as senator again in the daytime and still put in time making silver jewelry.

Instructor's Notes: Read each set of directions with students. Encourage students to use Review Word and Sight Word pages for practice writing sentences in a notebook or journal.

Syllables

A. Say the words aloud. Listen to the parts in each word. Some words have one part or syllable, and some have two syllables.

One Syllable	Two Syllables	
ranch	because	be-cause
time	silver	sil-ver
job	again	a-gain
works	person	per-son
put	people	peo-ple
drive	ago	a-go

B. Say each word aloud. Listen to the number of syllables in each word. Write the word under the correct heading.

law
problem
more
rancher
safety
father
group
country
own
like

One Syllable	Two Syllables
1. ____law____	1. ____problem____
2. _____	2. _____
3. _____	3. _____
4. _____	4. _____
5. _____	5. _____

C. Read the sentences. Draw one line under one-syllable words. Draw two lines under two-syllable words.

1. Ben Campbell holds down many jobs.

2. Campbell owns a horse ranch.

3. Sometimes he works with silver.

4. He puts in time working for people.

Instructor's Notes: Read each set of directions with students. Explain that each syllable always contains one vowel sound. Help students sound out syllables.

Phonics

Syllables and Schwa

A. Say the words aloud. Listen for the number of word parts you hear in each word. Each part is called a syllable. Each syllable has one vowel sound.

One Syllable	Two Syllables	Three Syllables
horse	own-er	fam-i-ly
been	man-y	sen-a-tor
hold	work-ing	jew-el-ry
life	Sen-ate	to-geth-er
things	quar-ter	e-lect-ed

B. Listen for how many syllables you hear in each word. Write the number.

wallet _____   different _____   someone _____

plan _____   learned _____   uniform _____

value _____   street _____   video _____

C. Listen for the vowel sound in the underlined syllables. This vowel sound is called the schwa. Each of the vowels— a̲, e̲, i̲, o̲, or u̲—can stand for the schwa sound.

a	e	i	o	u
a̲-bout	sil-ve̲r	fam-i̲-ly	lem-o̲n	cac-tu̲s

D. Listen for the schwa sound in each word. Write the letter that stands for the schwa sound.

again _____   doctor _____   parent _____

holiday _____   problem _____   person _____

Instructor's Notes: Read each set of directions with students. Help students sound out syllables in A and B. Explain that the schwa sound is shown in the dictionary by the symbol ə. Go over the examples for the schwa sound in C.

9

Unit 1

Back to the story...

Remember
What have you learned about Senator Campbell so far?

Predict
Look at the pictures. What do you think the rest of the story will be about?

One Man, Many Jobs: Ben Nighthorse Campbell

American Indians have been working with silver for some time. It takes time to learn to make jewelry well. Silver can be bent or it can be cut with a saw. The person working with silver can't take chances. Making silver jewelry is fine hand work.

Instructor's Notes: Read the questions with students. Help students review and predict. Then have students read the story silently. Use Blackline Master 4: The 5Ws Checklist from the *Instructor's Guide* to help students understand each story in this book. Have students keep their completed checklists in their notebooks or journals.

Many jewelry makers cut lines into the silver. On a clip or pin, they may cut lines that stand for the family that makes the jewelry. Senator Campbell likes to put horses on his jewelry because of his American Indian name, Ben Nighthorse, and his love for horses.

He sells a lot of his jewelry, but he gives some of it to groups of people who work for the same causes he does, helping American Indians and the land. Sometimes people tell Campbell what they want him to put on the jewelry he makes for them. Both men and women like and buy his silver jewelry.

Senator Campbell has been willing to take all the time needed to do a job well. He learned to make jewelry at the age of 12. He earned his G.E.D. and went on to get a B.A. using money he earned as a truck driver. He met different people and went to different lands on his own. Campbell worked with American Indians in prison to help them with the problems of coping with prison life. He wanted to help American Indians and all the people of the United States. He took action by running for senator and getting elected.

Campbell is a man who does many things well. He likes what he can do in his job as senator for people with problems. He feels he can use what he has learned from his own life in his job as senator. He likes the jewelry he makes with his own hands. He loves working with the horses on his ranch. Campbell's family helps him in his jobs when he isn't in the Senate. His wife helps him on the ranch, and his son helps him make jewelry. Making jewelry, running a ranch, and being a senator make up a good life for Ben Nighthorse Campbell.

Instructor's Notes: Have students describe some of the different things Campbell does in his life.

The time is right for an American Indian senator. There are many different groups in our country today. All of them want to have a say in how the country is run. People want senators who will stand up for them and work to get the laws they need. That's why Ben Nighthorse Campbell ran for the Senate and why many women were elected in 1992. All groups have the right to elect someone to the Senate who will see that their needs are met.

Senators talk with the people who elected them to find out if they are doing a good job. Senator Campbell likes talking to people as well as working on his ranch and making silver jewelry. He will keep doing all three jobs because he feels a life of action is the life for him.

Comprehension

Think About It

1. Why did people elect Campbell to be senator?

2. What do you know about the work a senator does?

3. What other work does Campbell do?

4. Sum up what makes Campbell a man of action.

Write About It

How could you benefit from having more than one job? How could having more than one job create problems?

Instructor's Notes: Help students read and answer the questions. Write About It can be used as a writing or discussion assignment.

12

Unit 1

Cause and Effect

When you ask, "Why did this happen?" you are looking for a **cause**.
When you ask, "What happened?" you are looking for an **effect**.

Example: He was elected senator because people like him.

                        effect   cause

Use these tips to find the cause or the effect.

1. Look for cause words such as the reason for, because, caused by, since, and why.

2. Look for effect words such as so and as a result.

A. Read the sentence and find the cause. Circle the number.

He puts horses on his jewelry

1. and works with horses on his ranch.

2. after he cuts the silver.

3. because of his name, Ben Nighthorse.

B. Read the sentence and find the effect. Circle the number.

He wanted to help people with problems

1. so he ran for senator.

2. and wanted to be a senator.

3. by talking to them.

C. Read the sentence. Underline the cause. Circle the effect.

Since Campbell is an American Indian, he took the name
Ben Nighthorse.

Instructor's Notes: Discuss the tips with students. Then read the directions with students.
Have students write sentences using cause and effect words in a notebook or journal.

Suffixes -ly and -y

A **suffix** is a word part added to the end of a word that changes the meaning of the word. The suffix -ly means "how something is done." The suffix -y means "full of" or "like." These suffixes are added to the words to describe people or things.

friend + ly = friendly   health + y = healthy

A. Add the suffix. Write the new word.

-ly	**-y**
1. different _____	**1.** need _____
2. love _____	**2.** hand _____
3. safe _____	**3.** hill _____
4. like _____	**4.** luck _____
5. night _____	**5.** might _____

B. Read the paragraph. Underline the words ending in the suffixes -ly or -y.

Campbell does things differently. He holds down more than one job, and he works for needy causes. The people are lucky that they elected him senator. His friendly ways are likely to get him elected again.

C. Write the word that fits best in each sentence.

lovely   handy   nightly   hilly

1. Campbell works on his jewelry _____ .

2. Isn't the silver jewelry _____ ?

3. Campbell is _____ at doing many things.

Instructor's Notes: Discuss the examples with students. Read each set of directions with students. For A, explain that suffixes add another syllable to each word. Have students read the new words formed.

D. Read the sentence. Write -ly or -y to complete the word.

1. Does he feel luck____ to be a senator?

2. They say he's a friend____ person.

3. His jewelry is fine____ made.

4. I'd like to be hand____ at making jewelry.

5. Ranching can be health____ work.

6. Some of the ranch is hill____ .

E. Write the correct word in each sentence.

1. (different, differently) The senator does things _____ .

2. (like, likely) He's not _____ to give up his jewelry work.

3. (luck, lucky) We're _____ to have a good senator.

4. (safely, safe) I hope he gets back _____ .

F. Write four sentences about someone you know who has two different jobs. In each sentence, use a word with an -ly or -y suffix.

_____

_____

_____

_____

Instructor's Notes: Read the directions together. Review the explanation and examples on page 14. Have students read their completed sentences aloud. For F, point out the icon in the margin and tell students it indicates a place for them to produce their own writing.

Writing a Letter

letter   government   Congress   signature

A. Read the words above. Then read the letter. Look at the five parts of the letter.

Inside Address —⟦ Senator Ben Nighthorse Campbell
Washington, D.C. 20510-0605

Greeting —⟦ Dear Senator Campbell,

Body —⟦   It was good to see you when you came to our city. I can tell by the way you talked to the people you met that you plan to help people with problems. We can use more senators like you on the job in our government. I hope you are elected again.

Closing ————⟦ Sincerely,

Signature ————⟦ *Dan Walters*

B. Match the parts of a letter to what each part tells you. Write the letter.

_____ **1.** inside address   **a.** your name

_____ **2.** closing   **b.** name and address of the person you're writing to

_____ **3.** signature   **c.** saying good-bye

C. Write a letter to your senator or congressman. Find the information you need to write the letter from one of the following places.

- Government listings in the telephone book
- Local newspaper
- Voter registration office in your area

Instructor's Notes: Read the new words and each set of directions with students. Go over the parts of a letter and explain the term *return address*. Help students find the information for C and assist them in writing a letter. Use the Unit 1 Review on page 17 to conclude the unit. Then assign *Reading for Today Workbook Four*, Unit 1.

Unit 1 Review

A. Write the word that best completes each sentence.

been	American Indian	elected	senator
ranch	silver	jewelry	again

1. Senator Campbell was _____ by the people.

2. He owns a _____ and makes _____ .

3. Ben Nighthorse is his _____ name.

4. Campbell may be elected _____ again.

B. Write the word under the correct heading.

lovely	letter	make	silver
congress	luck	worked	puts

One Syllable

1. _____

2. _____

3. _____

4. _____

Two Syllables

1. _____

2. _____

3. _____

4. _____

C. Write the word that fits best in each sentence.

1. The silver jewelry that Campbell makes is _____ .
                                             handy   lovely

2. He works on the jewelry _____ .
                            nightly   timely

3. Campbell gives time and money to _____ causes.
                                      mighty   needy

17

Unit 2 Using Coupons Effectively

Discussion

Remember

Look at the picture. Do you ever use coupons when you buy food?

Predict

Look at the picture and the story title. What do you think this story is about?

Do You Need to Buy It?

Nan: Say, Sis, what do we have to eat? I don't want to pay to eat out when I can eat at home.

Kay: Look up there and see. I get things all the time. I take a lot of time at the store finding good buys.

Nan: Well . . . I see eight cans of nuts, some hot dog buns, and a lot of pop. But these foods don't go together well. What is going on?

Kay: When I go to the store, I shop with these! They help me use my money well.

Nan: You are right. And these can help a lot when they are for things we need. But you are buying things that we don't need. You have to look at what we have. I don't like paying for something that we don't need.

Kay: I see. You want me to buy the things you want to eat, right? Maybe you need to do the shopping, Sis. That will help you see the problems I have to cope with!

The story continues.

Instructor's Notes: Read the discussion questions with students. Discuss the story title and the situation in the picture. Have students read silently. Have them underline words they don't recognize. Review the underlined words. Have students identify the speakers in the picture and their relationship to each other.

19

Unit 2

Review Words

A. Check the words you know.

☐ **1.** baseball ☐ **2.** game ☐ **3.** thing

☐ **4.** because ☐ **5.** many ☐ **6.** need

☐ **7.** buyer ☐ **8.** sell ☐ **9.** seven

☐ **10.** these ☐ **11.** see ☐ **12.** want

B. Read and write the sentences. Circle the review words.

1. Buyers like Kay want all the things they see.

_____

2. Do they buy because they need all these things?

_____

3. Kay doesn't need many of the things she buys.

_____

4. Store owners can make money when they sell to buyers like Kay.

_____

_____

C. Read the clues. Choose a review word for the answer.

1. a game played with a bat and ball _____

2. one more than six _____

3. something a child likes to play _____

Instructor's Notes: Read each set of directions with students. For A, have students read the
words aloud and then check known words. Have students practice any unknown words in a
notebook or journal.

Sight Words

could ● **coupon**
then ● **save**

A. Read the words above. Then read the sentence.

We **could** use **coupons** and **then save** money.

B. Underline the sight words in sentences 1–5.

1. I read the ads and then clip out the coupons.

2. Do I need to save all the coupons I see?

3. Could they help me save on something I need?

4. I could clip out the coupons I want to use.

5. Then I could use the coupons to get the things I need.

C. Write the word that best completes each sentence.

save   then   coupons   could

1. You _____ give me some tips about using coupons.

2. Cutting out _____ can take a lot of time.

3. Save a lot of coupons and _____ go shopping.

4. You don't _____ money if you buy things you don't need.

D. Read the sentences. Underline the sight words.

Nan and Kay want to save money when they shop. One way they could save money is to use coupons. Nan finds coupons in the store ads, and then Kay clips out the ones that could help them save. They save a lot of coupons and then buy the things they need.

Instructor's Notes: Read each set of directions with students. For A, read each sight word aloud. Have students repeat.

Sight Words
much ● **less**
think ● **cost**

A. Read the words above. Then read the sentence.

How **much less** do you **think** meat will **cost** with a coupon?

B. Underline the sight words in sentences 1–4.

1. Many people could pay less using coupons, but they don't think about it.

2. The right way to use coupons is to think about what you are buying.

3. How much money does meat cost without the coupon?

4. Will meat cost more or less at a different store?

C. Write the word that best completes each sentence.

much   less   cost   think

1. We use more coupons and pay _____ money.

2. I _____ the store will take our coupons.

3. How _____ meat do we need to buy?

4. Meat might _____ more at a different store.

D. Read the sentences. Underline the sight words.

Food costs more and more these days. I think we could save money by using coupons. But we have to think about some things when we shop. How much does food cost when we use coupons? Will the cost be less at a big store that has a lot of goods? How much trouble is it to get to that store?

Instructor's Notes: Read each set of directions with students. For A, read each sight word aloud. Have students repeat.

22

Unit 2

Sight Words

why ● roommate
spend ● too

A. Read the words above. Then read the sentence.

Why does my **roommate spend too** much money?

B. Underline the sight words in sentences 1–5.

1. My roommate saves all the coupons she sees.

2. Then she spends money for things we don't need.

3. When we shop together, she doesn't buy too much.

4. Why can't she do that when I'm not with her?

5. I think my roommate could learn to stop buying things we don't need.

C. Write the word that best completes each sentence.

too   roommate   why   spend

1. _____ do you think people save coupons?

2. Things cost _____ much money today.

3. I think that my _____ needs help shopping.

4. Why _____ more when you can save with coupons?

D. Read the sentences. Underline the sight words.

My roommate has a problem when she goes shopping without me. She spends money on things we don't need because she thinks she saves money. Then we have too many things, but not what we need. Why do store ads and coupons make people want things they can't use? I'm going to help my roommate quit buying things we don't need.

Instructor's Notes: Read each set of directions with students. Explain the different meanings of the words *to*, *too*, and *two*. Continue journal writing.

23

Unit 2

Consonant Blends with r

A. Listen to the beginning sound in each word. Underline the letters that stand for the r blend.

br	**cr**	**dr**	**fr**
brand	cream	drive	friend
brag	crop	drop	from

gr	**pr**	**tr**	**str**
group	problem	trouble	street
gray	prison	truck	strap

B. Make other words with r blends. Read and write the words.

-ay	**-ip**
gr + ay = _____	dr + ip = _____
fr + ay = _____	gr + ip = _____
tr + ay = _____	str + ip = _____
str + ay = _____	tr + ip = _____

C. Write the correct word in each sentence.

1. (bag, brag) Kay likes to _____ about the money she saves.

2. (trip, tip) Kay and I went on a big shopping

_____ .

3. (brand, band) She used a coupon to buy a good

_____ of hot dogs.

4. (ray, tray) We had a big _____ full of hot dogs to eat.

Instructor's Notes: Read each set of directions with students. For A, have students read the words aloud. Explain that the two consonant letters (three for *str*) blend together for the sound at the beginning of each word, but that students can still hear the consonant sound of each letter.

-y
why
by
my

A. Read the words on the left. Write other -y words.

cr + y = _____

dr + y = _____

fr + y = _____

tr + y = _____

B. Write a -y word to finish each sentence.

1. I think _____ roommate uses too many coupons when she shops.

2. Kay said she will _____ not to buy food we don't need.

3. _____ did she buy all these hot dogs?

-ink
think
pink
rink
sink

C. Read the words on the left. Write other -ink words.

w + ink= _____

br + ink= _____

dr + ink= _____

D. Write an -ink word to finish each sentence.

1. When I was a child, I liked to _____ pop.

2. My sister got 12 cans for us to _____ .

3. I don't _____ we needed that much pop.

Instructor's Notes: Explain to students that the -y stands for the long *i* sound in the known sight word *why* and many other one-syllable words ending in -y. Then show students the -ink word pattern in the known sight word *think*. The -ink words have the short *i* sound. Read each set of directions with students.

Remember

What has happened in the story so far?

Predict

Look at the picture. What do you think the women are doing? What do you think will happen in the rest of the story?

Do You Need to Buy It?

Kay: Nan, look at all these coupons! We could save big money this way. This is a good one . . . we buy seven cans of dog food and send in this coupon. Then they send us seven more cans!

Nan: That could be a good saving, but not for us, Kay. We don't have a dog!

Instructor's Notes: Read the questions with students. Help students review and predict. Have students read the story silently or ask students if they want to take parts in reading the story aloud.

26

Unit 2

Kay: OK . . . but this coupon is right for us. We can save ten cents on figs at the health food store. They cost much more at the store down the street.

Nan: Figs? Who likes figs in this home? What a roommate you are. You spend money on things we don't need because you think you are getting a good buy. It ends up costing us more money, not less money!

Kay: OK, Nan, I see why you don't want me to buy things we don't need. Good buyers don't use all the coupons they see. But I may need help from you, Sis.

Nan: Then give me these ads! I'll find some coupons we can use. Say! We could win tickets to a baseball game in May with this coupon. All we need to do is cut out the coupons from the hot dogs we buy and send them in. What do you think?

Kay: You don't have to sell me on baseball. I love ball games . . . and hot dogs, too.

Nan: We'll have to buy many, many hot dogs, Kay, because we need 50 coupons to win the tickets.

Many days go by . . . .

Kay: I don't think I like these hot dogs, Nan. Why don't we go out to eat?

Nan: We bought them to win the tickets for the baseball game. And we can't go out to eat because I spent all our food money on hot dogs.

Kay: But Nan, how much can a person spend on hot dogs? And how many hot dogs can we eat without getting sick? Well, you do think we'll win, don't you?

Nan: We'll win something because we did what the coupon said. What more could we do?

More days go by . . . .

Kay: Nan, look what came for us! It's from the coupon people, and I bet it's our tickets to the baseball game. I can tell this is our lucky day.

Nan: No! It can't be! Read this!

Kay: What is it, Nan? Did we lose?

Nan: We didn't lose, but we didn't win the baseball tickets. We're getting more hot dogs! They are on the way to us.

Kay: I think I'm going to be sick. I'm sick of seeing hot dogs and coupons. This has taught me the right way to use coupons. I found out that trying to save money can sometimes cost me money. I have to think about what I'm buying.

Comprehension

Think About It

1. Why did Kay and Nan have to eat so many hot dogs?
2. What did Kay and Nan win?
3. What did Kay learn about coupons?
4. Sum up what happened in the story.

Write About It

Do you think coupons are useful? Explain why or why not.

Instructor's Notes: Help students read and answer the questions. Write About It can be used as a writing or discussion assignment.

28

Unit 2

Inference

An **inference** is an idea you get by putting facts together.

Example: Jay saves his money. (Fact)

Then he buys tickets for baseball games. (Fact)

Jay likes baseball. (Inference)

Use these tips to make an inference.

1. Read the story.

2. List the facts that are stated.

3. Put the facts together to come up with your inference.

A. Read this paragraph.

Matt looked at the coupons. They were for tea bags. Matt gave the coupons to Kay. She used them when she went to the store.

B. List the facts.

Fact 1 _____

Fact 2 _____

Fact 3 _____

Fact 4 _____

C. Circle the inference you can make from the facts.

1. Matt saves coupons.

2. The coupons were no good.

3. Kay likes tea.

Instructor's Notes: Discuss the tips with students. Then read the directions together.

> **Add -ed to some verbs to show the past. For other verbs, change the spelling to show the past.**
>
> save saved   think thought
>
> **Examples:** I think of my sister. (I am doing it now.)
>
> I thought of my sister a lot. (I did it in the past.)

A. Read this list of verbs.

Present	Past	Present	Past
sell	sold	are	were
begin	began	find	found
give	gave	take	took
buy	bought	pay	paid
teach	taught	spend	spent

B. Read the paragraph. Underline the irregular verbs.

I gave some coupons to my roommate, and she took them to the store. Kay thought all the coupons were good, and she bought a lot of things. Then she found out the coupons were good in May, but not in June. I hope this taught Kay to read coupons well.

C. Complete each sentence by choosing the verb that tells about the past.

1. Someone at the store _____ my roommate a radio.

     sell   sold

2. The trouble was that Kay _____ too much for it.

     pay   paid

Instructor's Notes: Discuss the examples with students. Explain that irregular verbs show past tense by changing spelling instead of adding -d or -ed. Read each set of directions with students.

D. Write the past time verb that completes each sentence.

were   spent   began   taught   took

1. Kay _____ money on things she didn't need.

2. Nan _____ Kay something about coupons.

3. Some things on coupons _____ good buys.

4. Kay _____ to read the coupons closely.

5. She _____ the best coupons to the store.

E. Complete each sentence by choosing the verb that tells about the present.

1. Let's _____ some good coupons.
found   find

2. _____ me that one!
Give   Gave

3. Look, you can use it when you _____ food!
buy   bought

4. Yes, but you still _____ a lot for that food.
paid   pay

F. Write three sentences about buying things with coupons. Use a past time verb in each sentence.

_____

_____

_____

Instructor's Notes: Read the directions together. Review the examples on page 30. Have students read their completed sentences aloud.

31

Unit 2

longer   ounces (oz.)   word   expiration

A. Read the words above. Then read the coupons below.

1.

50¢   MANUFACTURER'S COUPON   NO EXPIRATION DATE

New!
Bright
LAUNDRY DETERGENT
171 oz.

SAVE 50¢
WHEN YOU BUY
ONE FAMILY SIZE (171 oz.)
OR THREE REGULAR SIZE (20 oz.)

9 780780 832671   50¢

2.

25¢   25¢

SAVE 25¢
on a 16-oz. package of
Good Times Hot Dogs

To the store owner:
Good Times Foods will give you the
value of this coupon and 7¢ for handling.
Customer will pay sales tax. This coupon
is good only on Good Times Hot Dogs.

HOT DOGS
GOOD TIMES
16oz.

25¢   MANUFACTURER'S COUPON
EXPIRES: 8/8/01   25¢

B. Read the questions and write the answers.

1. One of the coupons is good for a longer time. Is it coupon 1

or coupon 2? _____

2. What word does oz. stand for in both coupons?

_____

3. How much money can you save when you use each coupon?

coupon 1?_____ coupon 2? _____

Instructor's Notes: Read the new words and each set of directions with students. Read and
discuss the coupons with students. Use the Unit 2 Review on page 33 to conclude the unit.
Then assign *Reading for Today Workbook Four*, Unit 2.

32

Unit 2

A. Write the word that best completes each sentence.

roommate   save   less   cost
why   think   could   coupons

1. Cutting out _____ can take a lot of time.

2. _____ they help us save on something we need?

3. My _____ says that coupons can help us save money.

4. Do you _____ my roommate is right about coupons?

B. Write -ink or -y to make new words. Write the word that fits best in each sentence.

1. wh + _____ = _____   _____ did I buy all this pop?

2. dr + _____ = _____   I can't _____ all of it.

3. tr + _____ = _____   I'll _____ to take some back.

4. th + _____ = _____   Do you _____ the store will take some back?

C. Write the word that fits best in each sentence.

1. Who _____ my roommate a new radio?
   sell   sold

2. She _____ too much for it.
   paid   pay

3. It _____ me mad to find out what she _____ .
   make   made   spent   spend

Unit 3 Helping Children Learn to Read

Remember

Look at the picture. What feelings do you see in the people's faces?

Predict

Read the title. What is your answer to the question? What do you think this story is about?

Who Needs to Read?

Mr. Sanders is a man who has not learned to read. He has learned to get by in life. Someday he wants to take the time to have someone teach him to read. Something he wants more than that is for his son, Jay, to learn to read. He wants Jay's life to be different from his.

Jay has a problem with reading, too, but his family had not talked much about it. Then one night Jay told his dad that the teacher wanted to see his parents. It was time for the family to look into this problem.

When they sat at the table together that night, no one talked much. Jay looked down at his food without eating. The time to talk had come, but no one knew how to begin. When a father hasn't learned to read, how can he help his son learn?

The story continues.

Instructor's Notes: Read the discussion questions with students. Discuss the story title and the situation in the picture. Have students read silently. Have them underline words they don't recognize. Review the underlined words. Point out the title *Mr.* that is part of the name *Mr. Sanders.*

Review Words

A. Check the words you know.

☐ **1.** upset   ☐ **2.** teach   ☐ **3.** gave

☐ **4.** together   ☐ **5.** learn   ☐ **6.** said

☐ **7.** someone   ☐ **8.** take   ☐ **9.** down

☐ **10.** teacher   ☐ **11.** into   ☐ **12.** who

B. Read and write the sentences. Circle the review words.

1. Will Jay be upset because I can't teach him to read?

_____

2. I gave him help with baseball, but who will be his reading teacher?

_____

_____

3. When Jay takes time with his work, he does not get into trouble.

_____

_____

4. We'll all work together to help Jay learn to read.

_____

C. Match each review word and its meaning. Write the letter.

_____ **1.** down   **a.** a person

_____ **2.** said   **b.** not up

_____ **3.** someone   **c.** talked

Instructor's Notes: Read each set of directions with students. For A, have students read the words aloud and then check known words. Have students practice any unknown words in a notebook or journal.

Sight Words

mean • must
always • school

A. Read the words above. Then read the sentence.

Does this **mean** that Jay **must always** have trouble in **school**?

B. Underline the sight words in sentences 1–5.

1. Mr. Sanders always wanted to go to school.

2. Going to school means you have a chance to learn.

3. Schools are not always for children.

4. A teacher must spend a lot of time helping people learn.

5. Does our teacher mean that we must always do well?

C. Write the word that best completes each sentence.

must   always   mean   school

1. People don't have to go to _____ to learn.

2. Having a good teacher _____ helps you learn.

3. I _____ learn to read to help Jay.

4. Learning to read will _____ a chance for a good job.

D. Read the sentences. Underline the sight words.

Some parents think schools must always teach children to read. But children must get help at home with the things they learn at school. What does this mean for parents who can't read well? Sometimes these parents must get help, too.

Instructor's Notes: Read each set of directions with students. For A, read each sight word aloud. Have students repeat.

Sight Words

where ● meet
soon ● after

A. Read the words above. Then read the sentence.

Tell me **where** we can **meet soon after** school.

B. Underline the sight words in sentences 1–5.

1. Mr. Sanders must meet his son's teacher soon.

2. Jay told his father where to find the teacher.

3. Mrs. Keating said she will meet Mr. Sanders.

4. Soon he will talk to her about Jay's problem.

5. After this talk, Mr. Sanders will help Jay.

C. Write the word that best completes each sentence.

after   soon   where   meet

1. Parents can see teachers _____ school.

2. Many teachers save this time of the day to _____ with parents.

3. Can we meet with the teacher _____ ?

4. _____ can Mr. Sanders find Jay's teacher?

D. Read the sentences. Underline the sight words.

   Parents may have problems to work out when they meet with a teacher. They must find out where the school is. Sometimes both the child and parents must find a time to meet together with the teacher. Parents might need to be at home soon after work. But, when parents and teachers find time for these meetings, they can work out ways to help a child.

Instructor's Notes: Read each set of directions with students. For A, read each sight word aloud. Have students repeat. Point out the title *Mrs.* that is part of the name *Mrs. Keating.*

38

Unit 3

Sight Words

or ● grade
report ● card

A. Read the words above. Then read the sentence.

Did Jay get a good **or** bad **grade** on his **report card**?

B. Underline the sight words in sentences 1–5.

1. In school you may have to give a report.

2. Will you get a good or bad grade?

3. A report that makes the reader think will get a good grade.

4. Children don't get good grades on report cards because they are lucky.

5. Good grades mean the child did good work.

C. Write the word that best completes each sentence.

card   or   report   grade

1. The teacher will like Jay's _____ .

2. He will get a good _____ from the teacher.

3. Did Jay's parents see his report _____ ?

4. Were they glad _____ upset about his grades?

D. Read the sentences. Underline the sight words.

What does a good grade on a report card mean? It means the child did a lot of work to get the grade. Some children have trouble giving a report. A parent can help by talking with the child about what to say in the report, or they can spend time reading it together. Soon the child will get good grades on report cards.

Instructor's Notes: Read each set of directions with students. Continue journal writing.

Consonant Blends with s

A. Listen to the beginning sound in each word. Underline the letters that stand for the s blend.

sc	**sk**	**sl**	**sm**
scan	skin	slip	smoke
scold	sky	sled	smell

sn	**sp**	**st**	**sw**
snip	spend	stand	swim
snake	spell	store	sway

B. Make other words with s blends. Read and write the words.

-ay	**-y**
sl + ay = _____	sk + y = _____
st + ay = _____	sl + y = _____
sw+ ay = _____	sp + y = _____

C. Write the correct word in each sentence.

1. (sell, spell) Jay must learn to _____ and read well.

2. (say, stay) He will _____ after school to get help from his teacher.

3. (slip, sip) Jay won't let his grade _____ from a D to an F again.

4. (spend, send) Mr. Sanders wants to _____ time learning to read, too.

5. (sand, stand) Jay's parents will _____ by him and help him in school.

Instructor's Notes: Read each set of directions with students. For A, have students read the words aloud. Explain that the two consonant letters blend together for the sound at the beginning of each word, but that students can still hear the consonant sound of each letter.

A. Read the words on the left. Write other -eet words.

gr + eet = _____

sl + eet = _____

sw + eet = _____

-eet

meet

beet

feet

street

B. Write an -eet word to finish each sentence.

1. Mr. and Mrs. Sanders will go to Jay's school to

_____ his teacher.

2. His teacher is a _____ person who loves children.

3. She will _____ Mr. Sanders with a handshake.

C. Read the words on the left. Write other -ean words.

D + ean = _____

J + ean = _____

w + ean = _____

-ean

mean

bean

clean

lean

D. Write an -ean word to finish each sentence.

1. Jay's teacher is Mrs. _____ Keating.

2. She isn't a _____ teacher, but she makes Jay do his own work.

3. When Jay learns to read, he won't have to

_____ on his friends for help.

Instructor's Notes: Show students the *-eet* word pattern in the known sight word *meet*. Then show students the *-ean* word pattern in the known sight word *mean*. Explain that *-ee* and *-ea* both spell the long e sound. Read each set of directions with students.

Remember
What has happened in the story so far?

Predict
Look at the picture. How do you think the family is feeling? Describe what they are doing. What do you think will happen in the rest of the story?

Who Needs to Read?

They sat at the table together that night, but the Sanders family wasn't talking at all. Mr. Sanders didn't look at his son Jay. Jay looked down at his food without eating.

"Well, Jay, it looks like we've got trouble," his father said in a sad way. "How could you get this grade on a report card? It says you can't read. The teacher gave you an F in reading and spelling."

Instructor's Notes: Read the questions with students. Help students review and predict. Then have students read the story silently. Explain to students that this story takes place at the Sanders' home and at Jay's school.

"What can I say? I'm unlucky in school," Jay said. "Or maybe the teacher gave me a bad grade because she doesn't like me." Then Jay looked up at his father. "Dad, why must I learn to read? After all, you can't read, and you always get by OK."

Mr. Sanders could not say what he was feeling. All he could think about was how much he had always wanted to learn to read. When he was a child, he got a job and quit school. Then he was a family man. After that, he had no time for school.

"I can't tell you how much I want to read," he said. "A person who can't read is helpless at times. When I need to read something, I always have to get help from someone. You must learn to read, Jay."

"Well, my teacher wants to meet with you and Mother about the grades on my report card," Jay said.

A meeting with the teacher reminded Mr. Sanders of his own school days. He had many problems in his life then. To this day, talking about teachers, grades, and school still gave him trouble. But he wanted to help his son.

"I can go see her, but Mother needs to stay home with you," he said. "Where can I find the teacher?"

"She will be at the school tonight after seven," Jay said. "You can meet her in Room 10."

• • •

Mr. Sanders walked into Room 10 at a quarter after seven. A sweet-looking woman sat at the table. She looked up.

"I'm Mr. Sanders, Jay's father," he said. "I came about Jay's report card."

"Yes, Mr. Sanders. I was hoping you could come," the teacher greeted him. "I'm Jean Keating. Jay is having a lot of trouble in reading and spelling."

"Well, why don't you teach him to read?" Mr. Sanders said. "Isn't that a teacher's job?"

"Yes, but I must teach many children. Jay needs more help. He needs me at school and you at home."

Mr. Sanders looked down. He didn't want to tell her, but he must. "Mrs. Keating, I can't read. That is why I don't help Jay more. I always wanted to learn, but I don't know where to get help."

"There is a way you can help Jay. We work on reading here at the school two nights a week. Some people who come are parents like you. You'll find that you can learn in less time than you think."

"I need to do this for my son and for me. We can learn together. I'll have to work to keep up with Jay!"

Mrs. Keating laughed with Mr. Sanders. "Well, you can always get an A for being a good father."

Comprehension

Think About It

1. Why didn't Mr. Sanders learn to read long ago?
2. Why does he want to learn now?
3. What does Jean Keating suggest that Mr. Sanders do?
4. Sum up what happened in the story.

Write About It

What's hard about learning to read? What's fun about it?

Instructor's Notes: Help students read and answer the questions. Write About It can be used as a writing or discussion assignment. Discuss the kind of class Mr. Sanders will probably be attending at his son's school and other literacy programs for adults.

44

Unit 3

Stated Main Idea

> The **main idea** is the point the writer is making.
> **Use these tips to find the main idea.**
> **1.** Read the whole paragraph or story.
> **2.** Decide what the paragraph or story is about.
> **3.** Check the first part of the paragraph. Often, the main idea is stated there.

A. Choose the words that best complete each sentence. Circle the letter.

1. Jay isn't learning to read well because
   a. he is unlucky.
   b. he thinks he can get by without reading.
   c. his teacher is mean.

2. Jay's teacher can't spend more time with Jay because
   a. Jay has to work after school.
   b. she does not like him.
   c. she has many children to work with.

3. Mrs. Keating thinks that
   a. Jay's father is mean to Jay.
   b. Jay's father can help Jay.
   c. Jay's father needs a good job.

B. Circle the best choice for a new story title.

Parents Are Teachers, Too

Learning the Right Words

Children and Homework

Instructor's Notes: Discuss the tips with students. Then read the directions together. Explain that a story title often gives the reader the main idea of the story.

A **prefix** is a word part added to the front of a word. The prefix gives the word a new meaning. The prefix re- means "to do again." The prefix un- means "not."

re + do = redo   un + do = undo

A. Add the prefix and write each new word.

	re-		**un-**
1. read	_____	**1.** lucky	_____
2. mind	_____	**2.** sold	_____
3. pay	_____	**3.** clear	_____
4. run	_____	**4.** loved	_____

B. Read the paragraph. Underline the words with prefixes.

Jay thinks he is unlucky to have a teacher who makes him work a lot. But someday he will want to repay her for her help. The teacher tells Jay that he must reread things many times. She makes him redo work that has mistakes in it.

C. Write the word that best completes each sentence.

undo   remind   unclear   unloved

1. Sometimes what Jay reads is _____ .

2. I'll _____ my son to do his homework.

3. Jay will _____ all the teacher's work if he does not read at home.

4. Children who get bad grades may feel _____ .

Instructor's Notes: Discuss the examples with students. Read each set of directions with students. For A, have the students read the new words. Explain that prefixes add another syllable to each word.

D. Add the prefix. Then write the new word.

re-   **un-**

1. __re__ think _rethink_   1. ____done _____

2. ____teach _____   2. ____said _____

3. ____paid _____   3. ____safe _____

4. ____tell _____   4. ____hurt _____

E. Write the words from A or D that mean the following.

1. run again _____   2. not planned _____

3. not hurt _____   4. not sold _____

5. not said _____   6. teach again _____

7. tell again _____   8. think again _____

F. Write four sentences about learning to read. Use a re- or an un- word in each sentence.

_____

_____

_____

_____

_____

Instructor's Notes: Read the directions together. Review the examples and the explanation on page 46. Have students read aloud the words they write for D and E and the sentences they write for F.

47

Unit 3

 **Life Skills** **Reading a Report Card**

best   worst   name   math

A. Read the words above. Then read the report card below.

Student: Jay Benton Teacher: Jan Potts	**Pine Elementary** REPORT CARD			
SUBJECT AREAS				
	Reporting Periods			
	1	**2**	**3**	**4**
READING	B	C	C-	F
LANGUAGE	B	B	C	C
SPELLING	B	C	C-	F
MATHEMATICS	B	A	A-	A
CITIZENSHIP				
E = EXCELLENT S = SATISFACTORY I = IMPROVEMENT NEEDED U = UNSATISFACTORY				
	Reporting Periods			
	1	**2**	**3**	**4**
Follows directions	S	I	I	I
Completes assignments/homework	S	I	U	U
Turns work in on time	I	U	U	U

B. Read the questions and write the answers.

1. What did Jay make his best grade in?

_____

2. What was Jay's worst grade? What was it in?

_____

_____

3. Does Jay do his work on time in reading and spelling?
How do you know?

_____

_____

Instructor's Notes: Read the new words and each set of directions with students. Read and discuss the report card. Point out to students that *math* is a commonly used shortened form of the word *mathematics*. Help students answer the questions. Use the Unit 3 Review on page 49 to conclude the unit. Then assign *Reading for Today Workbook Four*, Unit 3.

Unit 3 Review

A. Write the word that best completes each sentence.

> always   after   means   report   must   grades

1. Mr. Sanders _____ wanted to learn to read well.

2. He wants Jay to get good _____ in reading.

3. That _____ Jay will have to do all his homework.

4. Jay _____ come home right _____ school.

B. Write -eet or -ean to make new words. Write the word that fits best in each sentence.

1. m + _____ = _____ Mr. Sanders will _____ Jay's teacher.

2. gr + _____ = _____ She will _____ him with a handshake.

3. J + _____ = _____ Jay's teacher is Mrs. _____ Keating.

4. m + _____ = _____ She isn't a _____ teacher.

C. Write the word that fits best in each sentence.

1. A person who can't read is _____ about some things.
     unclear   unloved

2. Jay must _____ things many times.
     rerun   reread

3. I'll _____ Jay to do his homework.
     repay   remind

4. Jay thinks he is _____ to have lots of homework.
     unlucky   unsold

Unit 4 Becoming a Parent

Discussion

Remember

Look at the picture. How would you feel if there was a new child coming into your family?

Predict

Look at the picture and the story title. What do you think this story is about?

A Family Man

What a lucky day this is for me! It's more like a holiday than a workday. Today Maria told me that I'm going to be a father! When she told me, I gave her a big hug. We wanted to both laugh and cry.

I must tell my family and friends. My parents will want to buy lots of things for the child. I bet they'll try to spend too much money. After the child comes, Maria's parents will drive up from the city to help out. Her best friend from down the street will go with her to the clinic.

We must think of a name for our child. Maria wants to name the child after her mother. I want a son to be named after my best friend. It's good that we have some time to think about a name.

I have a lot to learn about being a father, but my own father taught me a lot about being a loving parent. Maria will need my help with the heavy work at home. I'll take her to see the doctor, and I'll buy the right foods for her to eat. She must be in good health when the child comes. We're both smokers, but we'll quit for the child's sake. I'll do what I can to give this child a good life. I have big hopes for this family.

The story continues.

Instructor's Notes: Read the discussion questions with students. Discuss the story title and the situation in the picture. Introduce the proper name *Maria*. Help students pronounce the name. Have students read silently. Have them underline words they don't recognize. Review the underlined words. Have students identify the speaker.

A. Check the words you know.

☐ **1.** child ☐ **2.** come ☐ **3.** clinic

☐ **4.** doctor ☐ **5.** hope ☐ **6.** smoker

☐ **7.** drive ☐ **8.** hug ☐ **9.** parents

☐ **10.** heavy ☐ **11.** up ☐ **12.** street

B. Read and write the sentences. Circle the review words.

1. I gave Maria a hug when I learned about our child.

_____

2. The doctor at the clinic said our child will come in June.

_____

_____

3. I'm a heavy smoker, but I hope to quit soon for our child's sake.

_____

_____

C. Choose review words to complete the puzzle.

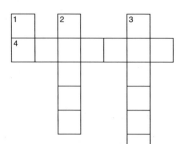

Down
1. not down
2. a trip in a car
3. a road

Across
4. mother
and father

Instructor's Notes: Read each set of directions with students. For A, have students read the words aloud and then check known words. Have students practice any unknown words in a notebook or journal. Explain to students that most crossword puzzles list words down, or *vertically*, and across, or *horizontally*.

Sight Words

as ● responsible
wife ● baby

A. Read the words above. Then read the sentence.

As responsible parents, my **wife** and I will both look after our **baby**.

B. Underline the sight words in sentences 1–5.

1. My wife Maria is doing what the doctor told her.

2. We're learning how to be responsible parents.

3. My wife stopped smoking because it isn't good for the baby.

4. As a mother-to-be, she must think of her health.

5. Responsible parents always try to make a good life for their children.

C. Write the word that best completes each sentence.

wife   as   responsible   baby

1. My _____ and I will soon be parents.

2. Having a _____ means a lot to us.

3. We want to be _____ parents.

4. We'll try to spend _____ much time _____ we can with our child.

D. Read the sentences. Underline the sight words.

After my wife found out she was going to have a baby, we both stopped smoking. We're responsible for our baby's health. As our child gets big, we'll feel responsible for the child's schooling as well.

Instructor's Notes: Read each set of directions with students. For A, read each sight word aloud. Have students repeat. Explain that *mother-to-be* is another kind of compound word.

Sight Words

before ● new
know ● small

A. Read the words above. Then read the sentence.

Before I'm a **new** father, I must **know** some things about **small** children.

B. Underline the sight words in sentences 1–5.

1. Before you know it, we'll have a new baby.

2. Do you think the baby will know that I'm a new father?

3. To be a good father, I must learn many new things.

4. I need to know how to carry a small child.

5. What do new parents feed a small baby?

C. Write the word that best completes each sentence.

small   know   new   before

1. _____ our baby comes, I need to learn how to be a good father.

2. Is there a school for _____ parents?

3. We need to _____ a lot of things.

4. _____ children need lots of help.

D. Read the sentences. Underline the sight words.

We have a lot to think about before the baby comes. My wife and I will be responsible for a new life. Does a small child cry all night? Will I need to spend more time at home than I did before? We know our lives are going to be different, but we feel good about a new baby in our family.

Instructor's Notes: Read each set of directions with students. For A, read each sight word aloud. Have students repeat. Go over with students the differences between *new* and *knew* and then *know* and *no*.

54

Unit 4

Sight Words

**pregnant ● tired
rock ● late**

A. Read the words above. Then read the sentences.

A **pregnant** woman may feel **tired** at times.
We will **rock** our baby **late** into the night.

B. Underline the sight words in sentences 1–4.

1. Maria's best friend Jan is pregnant, too.

2. Jan tells Maria that all pregnant women don't feel tired.

3. She rocks the baby to stop it from crying.

4. Jan says that new parents may feel tired from getting up
late at night to feed the baby.

C. Write the word that best completes each sentence.

tired   rock   late   pregnant

1. Get to the clinic before it's too _____ !

2. Dad used to _____ me when I was small.

3. Can a new father and mother get _____ ?

4. A group of _____ women meets at the clinic.

D. Read the sentences. Underline the sight words.

Maria was feeling tired, and she went to see the doctor. That
was when she found out she is pregnant. I came home late that
night, but she was up to tell me the good news. As soon as the
baby comes, I want to spend time rocking our baby.

Instructor's Notes: Read each set of directions with students. Review contractions used on
Sight Word pages. Continue journal writing. Review the uses of the period, the question mark,
and the exclamation mark in writing sentences.

Consonant Blends with l

A. Listen to the beginning sound in each word. Underline the letters that stand for the l blend.

bl	**cl**	**fl**
blend	clinic	fly
blink	clan	flag

gl	**pl**	**sl**
glad	player	sly
gland	plan	sleet

B. Make other words with l blends. Read and write the words.

-ink	**-ight**
bl + ink= _____	bl+ ight = _____
cl + ink= _____	fl + ight = _____
pl + ink= _____	pl+ ight = _____
sl + ink= _____	sl + ight = _____

C. Write the correct word in each sentence.

1. (pan, plan) We need to _____ a name for the baby.

2. (plight, light) Staying up all night to rock the baby is the _____ of new parents.

3. (lad, glad) We're _____ that we'll have the chance to be good parents.

Instructor's Notes: Read each set of directions with students. For A, have students read the words aloud. Explain that the two consonant letters blend together for the sound at the beginning of each word, but that students can still hear the consonant sound of each letter.

-ock and -ate

A. Read the words on the left. Write other -ock words.

bl + ock = _____

cl + ock = _____

sm + ock = _____

-ock

rock

lock

mock

sock

B. Write an -ock word to finish each sentence.

1. Carlos plans to _____ the baby at night.

2. Maria got a big _____ to fit her.

3. Carlos looks at the _____ . Is it time to go to the clinic?

4. Our baby will play with the _____ we made.

C. Read the words on the left. Write other -ate words.

pl + ate = _____

sk + ate = _____

st + ate = _____

-ate

late

date

gate

rate

D. Make an -ate word to finish each sentence.

1. I hope that our baby won't wake up _____ at night.

2. We have a _____ to see the doctor today.

3. The baby won't eat from a _____ for some time.

4. We can get a good _____ when we buy baby food.

Instructor's Notes: Explain that the *o* stands for the short vowel sound and the *ck* stands for one sound *(k)* in the known sight word *rock*. For the *-ate* words, explain that the *a* stands for the long vowel sound in the *a* + consonant + *e* pattern in the known sight word *late*. Read each set of directions with students.

Back to the story...

Remember

What has happened in the story so far?

Predict

Look at the picture. What do you think will happen in the rest of the story?

A Family Man

Maria: Carlos, before the end of the day, we'll be new parents. I can't help thinking about the day we found out I was pregnant.

Carlos: We were both glad, and our families were, too. How are you feeling? Do you want me to call the clinic and tell the doctor we'll be right there?

Maria: No, it's not time yet. You know, Carlos, we have not thought of a name for the baby. We'll need to have a name soon.

Instructor's Notes: Read the questions with students. Help students review and predict. Explain that *Carlos* is the name of Maria's husband in the story. Have students read the story silently or ask students if they want to take parts in reading the story aloud.

Carlos: I know . . . but I can't think of the right one. All I can think of is you. I hope that you don't have problems when the baby comes.

Maria: The doctor says the baby and I are both fine. I did as I was told at the clinic. I walked up and down our street two times a day. I didn't carry heavy things or get too tired. And I did not drive the car on big trips. The chances are good that I'll have no trouble when the baby comes.

Carlos: The doctor says it's a good thing that we stopped smoking when we learned that you are pregnant. When parents are smokers, small children in the home can get sick. As responsible parents, we had to quit.

Maria, I have big plans for this child. I've stocked our home with baby food and lots of small playthings. My brother lent us a baby bed. The baby will be in our room, with a rocker for us to sit in when we rock the baby. I hope we can be responsible parents, like our parents were for us.

Maria: I know that we can be, Carlos, but having a small child won't be all fun. Babies cry at all times of the day and night, and they have to be fed on time. New mothers and fathers feel tired a lot. Yes, this is going to be a new way of life for us.

Carlos: I'm lucky to have a wife who knows a lot about having a family. When you were a child, you had small brothers and sisters at home. That will help us both.

Maria: You know, there will be many times when our baby will need our help. We'll have to teach our child right from wrong. Children need help from parents to do well in school. And they need lots of hugs!

Carlos: It's a lot of work to be a responsible parent, but it will be fun, too. It will feel good to see our child learn to walk and talk. When our baby wakes up late at night, I'll be there to help you rock the baby. I hope this child gets here soon.

Maria: Carlos . . . I think you are going to get what you want. You must drive me to the clinic . . .

Carlos: Doctor! My wife is about to have the baby. We'll meet you at the clinic. Don't be late!

Comprehension

Think About It

1. Are Carlos and Maria glad about the baby? How do you know?
2. How will their lives change when the baby comes?
3. How will both parents help with the baby?
4. Sum up what happened in the story.

Write About It

How do the lives of a family change when a baby is born? Explain if the changes or good or bad, or both.

Instructor's Notes: Help students read and answer the questions. Write About It can be used as a writing or discussion assignment.

60

Unit 4

Comprehension   Implied Main Idea

A **main idea** is the main point the writer is making. If the main idea is not stated, we say it is implied. Then it's up to you, the reader, to find it. **Use these tips to find an implied main idea.**

1. Read the whole paragraph or story.
2. Decide what one main point all the sentences add up to. This is your clue to the implied main idea.

A. Read this paragraph.

Carlos and Maria want to be good parents. They learned from their own parents how to be responsible and loving. When the baby gets here, Carlos and Maria will both help tend the child.

B. Pick the best implied main idea. Circle it.

1. Carlos and Maria will be responsible parents.

2. Carlos and Maria will get their parents to tend the baby.

3. The baby will have a lot of fun.

C. Circle the best choice for a new story title.

How to Pick a Good Doctor

Maria and Carlos

Responsible Parents

Instructor's Notes: Discuss the tips with students. Go over the difference between the *stated* main idea and the *implied* main idea. Then read the directions together.

Adding -ies or -s to Words Ending in -y

We add s to some words to mean more than one. If a word ends in a consonant plus y, like baby, we usually change the y to i and add -es: babies.

baby = babies   cry = cries

A. Read the words. Then change the y to i and add -es. Read and write the new word.

1. family _____   2. cry _____

3. city _____   4. try _____

5. baby _____   6. country _____

B. Read the paragraph. Underline the words that end in -ies.

   Maria's parents and mine are from different countries. They came to this country, but they are in different cities. Our families did not meet before our wedding.

C. Write the word that best completes each sentence.

   cries   babies   tries   countries   families

1. Our _____ will be glad about the baby.

2. When the baby _____ , we pick her up.

3. Maria _____ to make the baby feel safe.

4. All new _____ need a lot of care.

5. Many _____ have laws that help children.

Instructor's Notes: Discuss the examples and the explanation with students. Explain that many words ending in y change the y to i and then add -es to form the plural. If necessary, point out the consonant letters on an alphabet chart. Read each set of directions with students.

62

Unit 4

> If a word ends in a vowel plus <u>y</u>, like day, we usually just add -s: days.
>
> day = days   boy = boys   key = keys

D. Add -s to the following words. Read all the words.

1. key _____

2. stay _____

3. toy _____

4. pay _____

5. day _____

6. play _____

E. Add -s or -ies to the word for each sentence. Write the word.

1. (family) Will our _____ help us with the new baby?

2. (stay) My mother _____ with us from time to time.

3. (toy) She sent some _____ for the new baby.

4. (boy) Most of the toys are for baby _____ .

5. (play) Sometimes Maria _____ with the toys just for fun.

6. (try) She _____ to get me to play with them, too!

F. What do you think are the best rules for taking care of a baby? Write your rules. Use some of your words from A on page 62 and from D on this page.

_____

_____

_____

Instructor's Notes: Read the examples and explanation with students. Point out that words ending in *y* with a vowel before the *y* do not change *y* to *i*. Read each set of directions with students.

Reading a Prescription

| tablets | should | daily | bottle |

A. Read the words above. Then read the label.

```
┌─────────────────────────────────────────────────────────────┐
│  A & B PHARMACY              THE PRESCRIPTION CENTER          │
│                                                               │
│   3005 S LAMAR                      PH. 555-7534              │
│   AUSTIN, TX                                                  │
│   6330237                                                     │
│                       DR. Hahn                                │
│                                                               │
│   MARIA GARCIA                                                │
│   TAKE ONE TABLET DAILY                                       │
│                                                               │
│   FERO-FOLIC  500 FILMTABS                                    │
│   ABBOTT / ROSS                                               │
│   STO1554                                                     │
│   02/20/01            QTY 100         REFILLS  CALL           │
└─────────────────────────────────────────────────────────────┘
```

CAUTION: FEDERAL LAW PROHIBITS THE TRANSFER OF THIS DRUG TO ANY PERSON OTHER THAN THE PATIENT FOR WHOM IT WAS PRESCRIBED.

B. Read the questions and write the answers.

1. How many of these tablets should Maria take daily?

_____

2. What should Maria do to get more of these tablets?

_____

3. How many tablets are in the bottle? How do you know that?

_____

4. The doctor gave Maria these tablets because she was feeling tired. Maria's father has been feeling tired, too. Should he take some of Maria's tablets? Why or why not?

_____

_____

Instructor's Notes: Read the new words and each set of directions with students. Read and discuss the label with students. Help students answer the questions. Use the Unit 4 Review on page 65 to conclude the unit. Then assign *Reading for Today Workbook Four*, Unit 4.

A. Write the word that best completes each sentence.

tired	before	new	pregnant
wife	baby	as	responsible

1. My _____ and I will soon be parents.

2. We're both _____ for looking after the baby.

3. _____ the baby comes, I'll need to learn many things.

4. Is there a school for _____ parents?

B. Write -ate or -ock to make new words. Write the word that fits best in each sentence.

1. pl + _____ = _____ A new baby can't eat from a

   _____ .

2. bl + _____ = _____ Babies like to play with the red

   _____ .

3. l + _____ = _____ Will Carlos have to get up

   _____ at night?

4. r + _____ = _____ He may have to

   _____ the baby.

C. Add -ies to the word for each sentence. Write the word.

1. (family) We know that our _____ will love the baby.

2. (cry) We won't mind when the baby's _____ wake us.

3. (baby) Someday we want to have more _____ .

Unit 5 *Understanding Others*

Getting to Know You

It was a hot day in June, and the Baker family was on its way to Sun Lake. Many people seemed to be going the same way. Cars and trucks were full of families out to have fun by the lake.

"Look at the people in that car!" said Jack Baker. "Who are they? They don't come from around here. You can tell that just by looking at them. What are they doing here?"

Kate Baker gave Jack a mad look. "You talk like that too much," she said. "It's not good for Reed and Nell. Our kids don't need to think like you do about how people are different."

"Right, Dad," said Nell. "We have kids in our school from a lot of different countries. They're just kids, the same as we are."

Reed said, "Dad, you talk like an old, old man who doesn't keep up with things."

"You'll find out when you get older. It's best to be with people who are your own kind," said Jack

The story continues.

Instructor's Notes: Read the discussion questions with students. Discuss the signs and the situation in the picture and the story title. Have students read the story beginning silently or together. Have them underline words they don't recognize. Review the underlined words.

67

Unit 5

Review Words

A. Check the words you know.

- ☐ **1.** bag
- ☐ **2.** player
- ☐ **3.** food
- ☐ **4.** truck
- ☐ **5.** same
- ☐ **6.** him
- ☐ **7.** took
- ☐ **8.** Kate
- ☐ **9.** different
- ☐ **10.** camera
- ☐ **11.** tape
- ☐ **12.** day

B. Read and write the sentences. Circle the review words.

1. One day, Jack and Kate took the kids to the lake in their truck.

_____

_____

2. They had a bag of food, a tape player, and a camera.

_____

_____

3. We are not all the same, but Jack doesn't like people who are different from him.

_____

_____

C. Match the word with its opposite. Write the letter.

_____ **1.** same   **a.** gave

_____ **2.** day   **b.** night

_____ **3.** took   **c.** different

_____ **4.** him   **d.** her

Instructor's Notes: Read each set of directions with students. For A, have students read the words aloud and then check known words. Have students add any unknown words to their notebook or journal and practice them.

Sight Words

summer • saw
foreign • around

A. Read the words above. Then read the sentence.

This **summer** we **saw** many **foreign** cars **around** the city.

B. Underline the sight words in sentences 1–3.

1. Some friends of mine went to a foreign country this summer.

2. They did not know how to get around and had trouble talking to the people there.

3. As soon as they could get around, my friends saw a lot of the city.

C. Write the word that best completes each sentence.

saw   summer   foreign   around

1. _____ is a good time to take a trip.

2. Have you been to a _____ country?

3. On our trip we _____ a lot of new sights.

4. Some people like to take trips where they can go _____ together in a small group.

D. Read the sentences. Underline the sight words.

When my family came to this country, it was a foreign land to them. They did not know how to get around in a big city. They were not used to the hot summers. Things were different for them, but they saw this foreign land as a chance for a new life.

Instructor's Notes: Read each set of directions with students. For A, read each sight word aloud. Have students repeat. Point out that the *g* in *foreign* is silent, and *ei* is pronounced like the short *i* in *win*.

69

Unit 5

Sight Words

thank ● park
snacks ● picnic

A. Read the words above. Then read the sentence.

We **thank** Mom for the **snacks** she made for our **picnic** in the **park**.

B. Underline the sight words in sentences 1–4.

1. We ate different snacks at our picnic.

2. Thank you, Mom, for all these snacks.

3. The bugs at the park liked our picnic, too.

4. After all, what is a park picnic without a bug or two?

C. Write the word that best completes each sentence.

thank   park   snacks   picnic

1. This summer we had a big family _____ .

2. It's a lot of work to make _____ for the family.

3. We need to _____ the person who made them.

4. A lot of people are around us in the _____ .

D. Read the sentences. Underline the sight words.

This summer we had a family picnic in the park. The sun was out all day, and the food was good. We ate snacks, played baseball, and talked. My mother made all the food for the picnic. Did we thank her for all these snacks?

Instructor's Notes: Read each set of directions with students. For A, read each sight word aloud and have students repeat it.

Sight Words

**newcomers ● language
grass ● jump**

A. Read the words above. Then read the sentences.

The kids play and **jump** in the **grass** with the **newcomers**. They don't seem to mind the different **languages**.

B. Underline the sight words in sentences 1–4.

1. Many newcomers go to the park in the summer.

2. Some of them use a different language.

3. All the children run and jump in the grass together.

4. The newcomers sit at a table by Jack and his family.

C. Write the word that best completes each sentence.

    jump   language   grass   newcomers

1. We didn't know the family of _____ .

2. They talk in a different _____ .

3. Nell and Reed wanted to _____ into the lake for a swim.

4. They ran over the _____ to the lake.

D. Read the sentences. Underline the sight words.

   People in the park may have different foreign languages. But they all like picnics and a swim in the lake. All the children like to run in the grass and jump into the cold water. Language isn't a problem for them. Reed, Nell, and the newcomers just yell and jump and have fun.

Instructor's Notes: Read each set of directions with students. Continue having students add words and sentences to their notebooks or journals.

71

Unit 5

Consonant Digraphs

A. Listen to the beginning sound in each word. Underline the letters that stand for the beginning sound.

ch	**sh**	**shr**
chance	shy	shrug
child	shake	shrink

th	**th**	**wh**
then	thank	when
that	thing	why

B. Make other words with ch, sh, shr, th, and wh. Read and write the words.

-in	**-ine**
ch + in = _____	sh + ine = _____
sh + in = _____	shr + ine = _____
th + in = _____	wh + ine = _____

C. Choose the correct word for each sentence.

1. (shrine, shine) The Baker family wanted the sun to

   _____ for their picnic.

2. (that, think) The Bakers had fun _____
   summer day.

3. (chin, chance) Reed hit his _____ on
   the rocks.

4. (wheat, whine) He was not hurt, and he did not

   _____ .

5. (thank, thin) Did Reed and Nell _____ their
   mom for the snacks?

Instructor's Notes: Read each set of directions with students. For A, have students read the
words aloud and listen for the beginning sounds. Explain that certain consonant letters together
(ch, sh, wh, th, and shr) make new sounds. Explain that the th digraph stands for two different
sounds as in then and thank.

72

Unit 5

Phonics

-ack and -ank

-ack

snack

back

pack

sack

A. Read the words on the left. Write other -ack words.

bl + ack = _____

sh + ack = _____

st + ack = _____

tr + ack = _____

B. Write an -ack word to finish each sentence.

1. The Baker family will _____ a picnic bag.

2. They carry the food to the park in a big _____ .

3. They stack the bags in the back of the _____ truck.

4. They like to go _____ to the old tables by the lake.

-ank

thank

bank

sank

C. Read the words on the left. Write other -ank words.

bl + ank = _____

dr + ank = _____

fr + ank = _____

D. Write an -ank word to finish each sentence.

1. Mrs. Baker likes to sit by the _____ of the lake.

2. The children _____ cold water when they got hot.

3. Reed dropped his radio in the water and it

_____ .

Instructor's Notes: Show students the *-ack* word pattern in the known sight word *snack* and the *-ank* word pattern in the known sight word *thank*. Explain that both patterns have the short *a* sound. Read each set of directions with students.

Getting to Know You

It was a good day to have a picnic in the park. It was hot, and the Bakers were glad to be by the lake. Before a big family outing like this, Kate Baker always did a lot of shopping. She bought bags and bags of food, with lots of snacks for the children. They all liked music, so she had someone in the family take a tape player. As she always did, she reminded Jack to get the camera.

When they got to the park, Kate told Reed and Nell about the park rules. Jack told his children to come right back to the picnic table after swimming. Then Kate and Jack let the children run down to the dock and jump in the water. But they didn't let the children get out of sight.

The Bakers had always been lucky about getting one table by the lake. They liked that table because no other tables were around it. But this summer there were three new tables by the lake! When the Bakers got to the park, a new family was sitting at one of the tables. From the way they talked, the Bakers could tell they were newcomers.

"I don't like it," Jack said. "They don't talk like we do. What is that language? They are not from this country. I can always tell when someone isn't from around here. Why do these people come to Sun Lake City?"

Instructor's Notes: Read the questions with students. Help students review and predict. Then have students read the story silently.

Jack was mad about the new family, but his kids didn't feel that way. Nell and Reed ran around with the three new children. They yelled and played.

"I don't like it at all!" said Jack.

"Just let them be." said Kate. "The kids are just fine."

The trouble came when Jack called his children back from the lake. Jack saw that his son Reed was running and yelling. A man ran after Reed and held him down on the grass.

"What are you doing to my son?" Jack yelled. Was the newcomer trying to hurt Reed? Then Reed sat up on the grass and Jack saw tape on his hand.

"I fell and cut my hand. This man helped me," Reed said.

"Your child cut his hand on the top of a can," said the man. "It will mend soon. I'm a doctor at the clinic in the city, and I treat many children. He will be OK."

"We can help our own children," Jack said. "What gives you the right to treat my child?"

The helpful newcomer looked at Jack without talking. Then he said, "Maybe I don't have the right to treat this child as mine but, as a doctor, I'm responsible for doing something to help. You've been looking at us all day," he went on. "I know we look different from you, but we like the park, as you do. We like picnics, as you do. And we love children and want to help when they are in trouble. I can see you feel the same way."

Jack looked down. "You're right. I should thank you for helping Reed. Thank goodness you're a doctor! Will you shake my hand?"

"Yes," said the man, and they both laughed. After that, Kate took some food to the new family. All the children played around the tables. Jack could see that children sometimes know a lot more than parents do!

Comprehension

Think About It

1. How does Jack feel about people who are newcomers to this country?

2. Why does Jack get mad at the man who ran after his son?

3. Does Jack change his mind about newcomers? What makes you think so?

4. Sum up what happened in the story.

Write About It

Write about a newcomer's feelings. The newcomer can be you or someone else.

Instructor's Notes: Help students read and answer the questions. Write About It can be used as a writing or discussion assignment.

76

Unit 5

Comprehension Sequence

Sequence is about time. It means the 1-2-3 order in which things happen.

Use these tips to find the sequence of events in a story.

1. Look for time words like before, when, after, then, always, soon.

2. Look for words that end in -ed. They tell what happened in the past.

Example: The children jumped into the water.

A. Write 1, 2, and 3 to show the order things happened in the story.

_____ Reed fell and cut his hand.

_____ The Bakers saw a new family sitting at the picnic table.

_____ The Bakers got into the car and went to the park.

B. Choose the words that complete each sentence. Circle the letter.

1. Kate Baker bought picnic food for the family
- **a.** after they got to the park.
- **b.** before they got to the park.
- **c.** when they got to the park.

2. Jack Baker made friends with the newcomers
- **a.** after he talked to them.
- **b.** before he talked to them.
- **c.** when he first saw them.

Instructor's Notes: Discuss the tips with students. Explain that sequence is the same as arranging things in order or listing the steps in how to do something. Then read the directions together.

A suffix is a word part added to the end of a word that changes the meaning of the word. The suffix -ful usually means "filled with." Adding -ness to a word changes the word from a describing word to a naming word.

help + ful = helpful   good + ness = goodness

A. Add the suffix and write each new word.

-ness

1. still _____
2. neat _____
3. sad _____
4. sick _____
5. shy _____

-ful

1. thank _____
2. play _____
3. use _____
4. hand _____
5. hope _____

B. Read the paragraph. Underline the words with -ful and -ness.

I'm hopeful that we'll have a good day for our picnic. The children will be playful in the park. I've told them to be helpful when we get there. I'm glad that sickness didn't keep the family at home.

C. Write the word that best completes each sentence.

shyness   thankful   handful   stillness

1. Reed put a _____ of chips on his plate.

2. He has no problem with _____ when meeting new people.

3. We were all _____ for a fun day.

Instructor's Notes: Discuss the examples with students. Read each set of directions with students. For A, have students read the new words. Explain that suffixes add another syllable to each word.

78 Unit 5

D. Write -ful or -ness to complete the words in the paragraph.

The newcomer tried to be use_____ . He showed sad_____

when Jack yelled at him. But now Jack and the newcomer feel

hope_____ about one another.

E. Write a word with -ful or -ness to complete each sentence.

1. A person who is very neat shows _____ .

2. A person who likes to play a lot is _____ .

3. A lot of stuff in your hand is a _____ .

4. When things are very still, there is _____ .

F. Use a -ful or a -ness word to replace each underlined word. Write the new sentence.

1. Nell and Reed were full of hope that their dad would like the newcomers.

   _____

   _____

2. The children felt a lot of thanks when their dad and the newcomer made friends.

   _____

   _____

3. Reed got over his feeling of being shy.

   _____

Instructor's Notes: Read each set of directions to students. Review the examples and explanation on page 78. For E and F, have students read their sentences aloud.

79

Unit 5

A. Read the words. Then read the rules below.

sign   lifeguard   allowed   other   adults

PARK RULES

1. Sign in when you get here.
2. Children must mind the lifeguard at all times.
3. No children under 12 without adults.

4. No pets in the park.
5. No cars in the park after 10 P.M.
6. Do not litter.

B. Read the questions and write the answers.

1. Do most parks have rules? Why?

_____

_____

2. Which rules are made to keep people safe?

_____

3. Which rules are made to keep the park clean?

_____

4. What other park rules would you add?

_____

_____

Instructor's Notes: Read the new words and each set of directions with students. For B, read and discuss the park rules. Use the Unit 5 Review on page 81 to conclude the unit. Then assign *Reading for Today Workbook Four*, Unit 5.

A. Write the word that best completes each sentence.

park   foreign   language   grass   jump   newcomers

1. On a summer day, many people go to the _____ .

2. We see families we know and some _____ .

3. Some families use a _____ language.

4. All the children run, _____ , and play games.

B. Write **-ack** or **-ank** to make new words. Write the word that fits best in each sentence.

1. p + _____ = _____   The Baker family will _____ a picnic bag.

2. b + _____ = _____   They'll go _____ to the table by the lake.

3. th + _____ = _____   Did you _____ her for all this food?

4. b + _____ = _____   We can sit on the _____ of the lake.

C. Write the word that fits best in each sentence.

1. We were _____ the sun was out all day.
           hopeful   thankful

2. Thank _____ Dad has a big van.
         goodness   sickness

3. I'm lucky to have _____ children.
          handful   helpful

Unit 6 *Overcoming Shyness*

Discussion
Remember
Look at the picture.
Do you usually enjoy
yourself at parties?

Predict
Look at the picture and the
story title. What do you
think this story is about?

Lonely in a Group

I walk from room to room. Sometimes I carry a drink to have something to do with my hands. People walk by me and say, "How are you?" I say, "Fine," but I don't mean it. They might think I'm having a good time, but I'm faking it. I feel shy and lonely.

I don't know one person here but my wife. Unlike me, she knows many people, and they all like her. I can see her laughing and chatting with her boss and some of her friends. I think they are talking about things at work.

I have trouble trying to talk with people I don't know. I feel differently when I'm with my own friends. I feel at home with them because I know they like me.

My wife says that learning to be a good talker is a skill. She tells me not to give up on this problem, but does she know what it's like to be shy? It's like walking down a road with no end in sight. But in time, maybe I'll find a way to get over this problem.

The story continues.

Instructor's Notes: Read the discussion questions with students. Discuss the story title and the situation in the picture. Have students read silently. Have them underline words they don't recognize. Review the underlined words. Have students identify the speaker.

A. Check the words you know.

☐ 1. road   ☐ 2. sometimes   ☐ 3. fine

☐ 4. give   ☐ 5. lonely   ☐ 6. own

☐ 7. wife   ☐ 8. problem   ☐ 9. carry

☐ 10. does   ☐ 11. talker   ☐ 12. person

B. Read and write the sentences. Circle the review words.

1. Sometimes I have problems talking to a person I don't know.

_____

_____

2. My own wife tells me I can be a fine talker, but it does not help me.

_____

_____

3. Being in a big group gives me a lonely feeling.

_____

_____

C. Choose review words to complete the puzzle.

Across
1. take from one spot to another
3. one who talks
Down
2. a street

Instructor's Notes: Read each set of directions with students. For A, have students read the words aloud and then check known words. Have students practice any unknown words in a notebook or journal.

84

Unit 6

Sight Words

ask ● over
would ● better

A. Read the words above. Then read the sentences.

I'll **ask** my friend Fran to help me get **over** this problem.
Then I **would** feel **better** about being in big groups.

B. Underline the sight words in sentences 1–4.

1. I would like to be a better talker.

2. Who can I ask to help me get over this problem?

3. I can ask my friend Fran to help me.

4. I could not ask for a better friend than Fran.

C. Write the word that best completes each sentence.

ask   would   over   better

1. I _____ like to have a good time in a group of new people.

2. I can _____ Fran to help me learn how to make new friends.

3. I'll get _____ tips from her.

4. Fran can help me get _____ feeling lonely in a big group.

D. Read the sentences. Underline the sight words.

Would you feel lonely in a big group of people? I would. Fran says I'd better learn to talk. Over and over again she tells me this, "Walk around and soon you'll meet a person who would like to chat."

Instructor's Notes: Read each set of directions with students. For A, read each sight word aloud. Have students repeat.

Sight Words

bring ● every
party ● never

A. Read the words above. Then read the sentence.

My wife **brings** me to **every party**, but I **never** feel like part of the group.

B. Underline the sight words in sentences 1–5.

1. My wife likes to go to every party, big or small.

2. I never want to go to a party where there are lots of people.

3. When I meet new people, I never know what to say.

4. I always feel better when I can bring my wife.

5. For a shy person like me, every party is lonely.

C. Write the word that best completes each sentence.

party   every   bring   never

1. I _____ like big parties.

2. I feel like _____ other person here is having a good time.

3. There are a lot of good snacks at this _____ .

4. What snacks did my wife _____ ?

D. Read the sentences. Underline the sight words.

When I'm at a big party, I would like to feel better than I do. Every other person seems to be having a good time, but I'm faking it. Being around people I don't know brings out my shyness. I never know the right thing to say. Does a big party make you feel this way?

Instructor's Notes: Read each set of directions with students. For A, read each sight word aloud. Have students repeat.

86

Unit 6

Sight Words

join ● company
belong ● club

A. **Read the words above. Then read the sentences.**

I don't **join** the group at my wife's **company** party because I feel that I don't **belong**. It's like a **club**.

B. **Underline the sight words in sentences 1–5.**

1. My wife's company gives a big party on a holiday.

2. She always asks me to join her friends from work.

3. They talk about people and things from the company.

4. Because I don't know what they are talking about, I feel that I don't belong there.

5. I must learn how to join the club.

C. **Write the word that best completes each sentence.**

belong   company   join   club

1. My wife works for a good _____ .

2. All the workers feel that they _____ .

3. It's much like joining a _____ .

4. But when you don't work there, you can't always _____ the group.

D. **Read the sentences. Underline the sight words.**

When my wife's company gives a party, I don't have a good time. I feel like I'm on my own, that I don't belong to the group. I don't know how to join in the fun. Why do I feel that they have a club and I don't belong to it?

Instructor's Notes: Read each set of directions with students. Continue journal writing.

Silent Letters

A. Listen to the sounds in each word. Underline each letter that stands for no sound, or is silent.

wr	**kn**	**gu**	**gh**
write	know	guitar	right
wrap	knit	guide	knight

B. Make other words with **kn** or **wr**. Read and write the words.

kn + it   = _____   wr + ote = _____

kn + ock = _____   wr + ing = _____

kn + ot   = _____   wr + y   = _____

kn + ight = _____   wr + ap = _____

kn + ee   = _____   wr + en = _____

C. Write the correct word in each sentence.

1. (knock, know) I don't _____ what to say to people at a party.

2. (wring, wrap) I stand at the back of the room and

   _____ my hands.

3. (knit, knee) I don't fit in with this tightly

   _____ group of people.

4. (wry, wrap) I hope they _____ up this party. I want to go home.

5. (right, write) I feel like I never say the _____ thing.

Instructor's Notes: Read each set of directions with students. For A, have students read the words aloud. Explain that in some words not all the letters stand for a sound. For example, in the *wr* pattern, the *r* is sounded and the *w* is silent. Students will need to learn to recognize silent letters.

88

Unit 6

A. Read the words on the left. Write other -ing words.

-ing
bring
king
ring
sing
wing

spr + ing = _____

str + ing = _____

sw + ing = _____

wr + ing = _____

B. Write an -ing word to finish each sentence.

1. Fran knows how to get into the _____ of things at a party.

2. She can _____ and play the guitar.

3. Fran likes to _____ friends to the party.

C. Read the words on the left. Write other -ub words.

-ub
club
hub
rub
tub

gr + ub = _____

shr + ub = _____

sn + ub = _____

D. Write an -ub word to finish each sentence.

1. How can I join this _____ ?

2. I feel that the people _____ me.

3. Fran is always at the _____ of the action at a party.

Instructor's Notes: Show students the *-ing* word pattern in the known sight word *bring* and the *-ub* word pattern in the known sight word *club*. Explain that both patterns have short vowel sounds (*i* and *u*). Read each set of directions with students.

Back to the story...

Remember
What has happened in the story so far?

Predict
Do you think a person can get over being shy? If so, how?

Lonely in a Group

Every time my wife's boss gives a company picnic or a party, I have a problem joining the group. Sometimes I feel that I don't belong with people I don't know. My wife knows that I hate going to these parties, but she always wants me to go with her. She is an outgoing person, and she can't see why I have trouble talking to people.

I must get over this problem. Then I would not be lonely in a group of new people. I would have a good time and feel that I belong in the company club.

I'll talk with my friend Fran about my shyness. Fran sells homes to people in our city, and she is used to talking to people she does not know. Fran can make friends right away with no trouble. You might say that it's one of her jobs to be a good talker.

• • •

"To make friends, Rick, you have to be a friend. You don't have problems when you are around people you know, do you?" Fran asked.

"No, but then I know they like me," I said. "I keep thinking about that company party. Over and over I couldn't think of the right thing to say. I never want to go back to one again."

"Tell me about it," said Fran. "Maybe I can give you some good tips that work for me."

Instructor's Notes: Read the questions with students. Help students review and predict. Then have students read the story silently.

"Sometimes I feel better when I have something to do with my hands. I carry a drink around with me, but at the other party, I spilled it all over the rug. When I try to think of the right thing to say, my mind is blank and the words don't come out right. See what I mean?" I asked.

"OK. Why don't we talk about some better ways to meet people at a party? When a person you don't know sits down by you, what do you say?" Fran asked.

"I try to give them a friendly greeting and tell them my name," I said.

"Is that all?"

"What do you want me to say?" I asked.

"Well, there are some things everyone wants to talk about. Ask about family, work, or school. Or a person may know a lot about something, like baseball or fine music. Another tip is to think about what you can give to a party. I know you can play the guitar well. Why not bring the guitar to the party and ask others to join in the singing? Or bring some games—people of all ages like games. When you are playing a game, you don't have time to think about what to say."

I need to think about Fran's tips. When I go to a party, it does not help to think about how shy I feel. I need to join in the fun, and then think less about my own problems. Every party would be a chance to meet new people. After all, there might be other people in the group who feel shy, too. Maybe we could make our own club!

After talking with Fran, I think I'm on the right road to overcoming my shyness. I'll never need to feel lonely in a group again.

Comprehension

Think About It

1. How does Rick feel when he goes to parties?

2. How is Rick's wife different from him?

3. What advice does Fran give Rick?

4. Sum up what happened in the story.

Write About It

When do you feel shy or lonely? What do you do to feel less shy or lonely?

Instructor's Notes: Help students read and answer the questions. Write About It can be used as a writing or discussion assignment.

Context

Using **context** means learning a new word by looking at all the other words in a sentence or paragraph. When you use context, you decide what does and doesn't fit with the other words.

Use these tips for using context.

1. Read the sentence to the end. Don't stop at the new word.

2. Think about what word makes sense.

A. Read the sentence. Answer the questions about the new word.

Fran will <u>invite</u> all her friends to her party.

1. Could it mean <u>remember</u>? _____
(Clue: That word would not make sense in the sentence.)

2. Could it mean <u>ask</u>? _____ (That makes sense.)

B. Read the paragraph. Use context to decide what the underlined words mean. Write what each word means.

Rick has trouble talking to people he does not know. You could say he is a <u>bashful</u> person. He can't think of the right things to say. Maybe these people won't like him. Maybe they would like to spend time with other friends. The more Rick thinks about these things, the more shy he becomes. He doesn't <u>enjoy</u> being shy.

1. A bashful person is _____ .
bossy   shy   tired

2. Enjoy means to _____ .
like   need   want

Instructor's Notes: Discuss the tips with students. Then read the directions together. Discuss how students can use context in reading any kind of material.

93

Unit 6

> An abbreviation is a short form of a word. Most abbreviations end with a period. An abbreviation that is part of the name of a person or place begins with a capital letter.
>
> Doctor = Dr.   Company = Co.

A. Read each word and its abbreviation. Write each abbreviation.

Street = St. _____   Road = Rd.   _____

Doctor = Dr. _____   Avenue = Ave.   _____

ounce = oz. _____   pound = lb.   _____

gram = g   _____   kilometer = km _____

B. Read the paragraph. Underline the abbreviations.

My wife works for the Clay Co. on Shell Ave. The company has a health plan with Dr. Parker. The doctor works at Pope St. and School Rd. I will see Dr. Parker at the company party on Sunday, June 4.

C. Draw lines to match the abbreviation with the word it stands for.

1. Rd.   company

2. Dr.   mister

3. Co.   avenue

4. Mr.   road

5. Ave.   doctor

Instructor's Notes: Discuss the examples and the explanation with students. Explain that the abbreviated form has the same meaning and pronunciation as the long form. For example, *St.* is read as *street*. Point out that *g* and *km* are metric abbreviations and do not end with a period. Read each set of directions with students and have them complete the activities.

94

Unit 6

D. Read each pair of phrases. Underline the one that is correct.

1. 24 Spring St.
24 Spring st.

2. Dr. and mrs. Gates
Dr. and Mrs. Gates

3. the Silver Ranch Co
the Silver Ranch Co.

4. 1 lb. and 2 oz.
1 lb. and 2 Oz.

E. Write the abbreviation for each title or word.

1. Doctor Key _____

2. Land Avenue _____

3. 25 grams _____

4. Dean Company _____

5. Dune Street _____

6. 5 kilometers _____

7. Waters Road _____

F. Write three sentences with abbreviations as shown:

1. A sentence with the name and title of a person

_____

2. A sentence with the name of a street

_____

3. A sentence with the name of a company

_____

Instructor's Notes: Read each set of directions with students. For F, discuss with students the sentences and abbreviations they will write.

Coping with Shyness

list   attention   relax   wrong

A. Read the words above. Then read the tips.

How to Cope with Shyness

1. Look right at a friendly face when you are talking before a group. Think about the worst mistake you could make and laugh about it. Ask "If I flub a line in my talk, will everyone get up and walk out? No!"

2. Don't make up for shyness by being bossy. You may not want others to know how you feel, but being bossy isn't good.

3. Get other people to talk. Then stop thinking about you and pay attention to what they are saying.

4. Don't make up for shyness by drinking too much. You may think it will help you talk, but you'll say the wrong thing.

5. Relax! There will be other shy people around. You are more like other people than you are different.

B. Read the questions and write the answers.

1. Most of the list tells you what to do about shyness. Which sentences tell you what not to do?

_____

2. Which three things in the list might be the most helpful to you? Why?

_____

_____

3. Tip 5 says, "You are more like other people than you are different." What does this sentence mean?

_____

_____

Instructor's Notes: Read the new words and each set of directions with students. Read and discuss the tips with students. Help students answer the questions. Use the Unit 6 Review on page 97 to conclude the unit. Then assign *Reading for Today Workbook Four*, Unit 6.

A. Write the word that best completes each sentence.

club   every   would   belong   over   bring   never

1. I _____ can relax at big parties.

2. I _____ like to have fun in a group of new people.

3. Somehow I feel like I don't _____ .

4. _____ time I try to say something, the words come out wrong.

B. Write -ub or -ing to make new words. Write the word that fits best in each sentence.

1. cl + _____ = _____ Why did I join this _____ ?

2. sn + _____ = _____ Maybe the people here will not

   _____ me.

3. sw + _____ = _____ I need to learn how to get in the

   _____ of things.

4. br + _____ = _____ Would it help to _____ some of my own friends?

C. Draw lines to match the words and abbreviations.

1. Street   oz.

2. kilometer   Dr.

3. Avenue   St.

4. ounces   Ave.

5. Doctor   km

Unit 7 Working Toward a Goal

Remember

Look at the picture. When do you discuss important goals with others?

Predict

Look at the picture and the story title. What kinds of goals do you think these people might be discussing?

No Problem with Problems

Jean spun around on her skates.

"Well done," said Nate. "You've been working on that."

"Right," said Jean. "I had trouble at first, but I didn't give up. I did it over and over."

Kim skated by on one foot. "Let's go around the park," she said. "I need a good workout."

The three friends talked as they went.

"I'm meeting with someone about a job," Jean told Nate and Kim. "It's at the Summer Company."

"That's a fine company," said Nate. "They have stores all over the country."

"Do you still have that tan dress with the black top?" asked Kim. "You look nice in it. It's the right kind of thing for going to a job."

"Is it better than the red and pink one?" asked Jean.

"Yes!" said Kim. "The red and pink one is too much. It's a party outfit. You should look neat and together for this meeting. You want the job, after all."

"OK," said Jean. "I want to do this right."

The story continues.

Instructor's Notes: Read the discussion questions with students. Discuss the story title and the photograph. Ask students how they solve problems. Have students read the page silently or together. Have students underline words they don't recognize. Review the underlined words. Have students name the three people in the story so far.

99

Unit 7

Review Words

A. Check the words you don't know.

☐ **1.** join   ☐ **2.** responsible   ☐ **3.** right

☐ **4.** company   ☐ **5.** about   ☐ **6.** list

☐ **7.** learn   ☐ **8.** new   ☐ **9.** problems

☐ **10.** when   ☐ **11.** want   ☐ **12.** should

B. Read and write the sentences. Circle the review words.

1. I would like to learn a responsible job and join a big company.

2. I know I need to look right when I go to a meeting about a new job.

3. I'll make a list of what I should do.

4. I don't want problems when I go to this meeting.

C. Read the clues. Choose a review word for the answer.

1. become part of   _____

2. find out   _____

3. not old   _____

4. troubles   _____

5. correct   _____

6. wish for   _____

Instructor's Notes: Read each set of directions with students. For A, have students read the words aloud and then check known words. Have students practice any unknown words in a notebook or journal.

Sight Words

now ● center
keep ● year

A. Read the words above. Then read the sentence.

At the job **center** they **now keep** new listings up all **year**.

B. Underline the new words in sentences 1–4.

1. Jean's school runs a job center.

2. Bill has worked at the center for a year.

3. He keeps telling Jean about new jobs.

4. Now she is going to talk to someone about a job.

C. Write the word that best completes each sentence.

now   center   keep   year

1. This has been a good _____ for Jean at school.

2. _____ she wants to find a job.

3. The people at the job _____ have helped her.

4. If Jean doesn't get this job, she will _____ looking.

D. Read the sentences. Underline the sight words.

Jean went to the center at the end of the school year. "Now is the time to get a job," she said. Jean wanted a responsible job that she could keep for many years. She talked to people at the center about what she could do. Jean will keep looking if this job doesn't work out.

Instructor's Notes: Read each set of directions with students. For A, read each sight word aloud and have students repeat it.

101

Unit 7

Sight Words

once ● listen
solve ● interview

A. Read the words above. Then read the sentences.

Bill said, "**Once** you are at an **interview**, let the person know what skills you have. Do you **listen** well? Can you **solve** problems?"

B. Underline the sight words in sentences 1–4.

1. Jean once had a job at a store.

2. Her interview is for a different job.

3. In this job she would have to solve many problems.

4. You need to listen to people to solve problems.

C. Write the word that best completes each sentence.

solve   listen   interview   once

1. When she was in school, Jean _____ had a weekend job she didn't like.

2. Her boss didn't _____ to Jean at that job.

3. Jean couldn't _____ this problem with the boss.

4. She hopes her _____ for a new job will go well.

D. Read the sentences. Underline the sight words.

Jean didn't know what an interview was like. "We can solve that," said Bill. "I'll help you with this upcoming interview." They went over things once and then once more. "Listen to what the person says," Bill told Jean. "And talk so he or she listens to you."

Instructor's Notes: Read each set of directions with students. For A, read each sight word aloud and have students repeat it.

102

Unit 7

Sight Words

straight ● career
careful ● customers

A. Read the words above. Then read the sentences.

Can Jean go **straight** from school into a **career**? She'll have to do a **careful** job and work well with **customers**.

B. Underline the sight words in sentences 1–4.

1. Jean wants to begin a career as a buyer.

2. She knows that she should be careful about how she looks.

3. Standing up straight will make her look better.

4. In this job Jean would have to know the company's customers.

C. Write the word that best completes each sentence.

customers   career   straight   careful

1. Sit up _____ at a job interview.

2. Ask about the company's _____ .

3. Be _____ when filling out the list of things you arc asked.

4. Tell why this _____ is good for you.

D. Read the sentences. Underline the sight words.

Where does a store get the things it sells to customers? Big stores have people called buyers who buy straight from the companies that make things. Jean wants a career at the Summer Company. At first she would help the jewelry buyer there. A buyer has to be very careful. If she buys the wrong things, customers might not like them.

Instructor's Notes: Read each set of directions with students. Continue journal writing.

A. Read the words and listen for the last vowel sound. Write the word and circle the letter that stands for the last sound.

why
baby
<u>y</u> = long i
<u>y</u> = long e

1. why _____   **1.** baby   _____

2. my _____   **2.** jewelry _____

3. shy _____   **3.** party _____

4. dry _____   **4.** lonely _____

B. Read the words. Then write each word under the right heading.

| sly | try | lucky | healthy |
| cry | many | heavy | fly |

<u>y</u> = long i   <u>y</u> = long e

1. _____   **1.** _____

2. _____   **2.** _____

3. _____   **3.** _____

4. _____   **4.** _____

C. Read the sentences. Circle the <u>y</u> words with the long <u>i</u> sound. Underline the <u>y</u> words with the long <u>e</u> sound.

I've had many jobs over the years. I'm lucky to have a chance to try a new company. My old job didn't work for me, but I know why. Now I can interview for a good career and make money at the same time.

Instructor's Notes: Read each set of directions with students. Explain that the *y* can stand for the long *i* sound at the end of one-syllable words or the long *e* sound at the end of words with more than one syllable.

-eep and -ear

A. Read the words on the left. Write other -eep words.

-eep

keep

jeep

deep

weep

sh + eep = _____

sl + eep = _____

st + eep = _____

sw+ eep = _____

B. Write an -eep word to finish each sentence.

1. Jean will work to _____ her new job.

2. The costs at the career center are _____ , and she doesn't have much money.

3. Now she must get her _____ and every night!

C. Read the words on the left. Write other -ear words.

-ear

year

dear

fear

hear

near

cl + ear = _____

sh + ear = _____

sm+ ear = _____

sp + ear = _____

D. Write an -ear word to finish each sentence.

1. The Summer Company is _____ my home.

2. I will listen well to _____ our customers.

3. It is _____ that I want a career as a jewelry buyer.

Instructor's Notes: Show students the *-eep* word pattern in the known sight word *keep* and the *-ear* word pattern in the known sight word *year*. Explain that both patterns have the long *e* vowel sound. Read each set of directions with students.

Remember
What has happened in the story so far?

Predict
Look at the picture. What do you think this has to do with Jean's job interview?

No Problem with Problems

Jean and her friends skated once around the park. They talked some more about Jean's interview.

"I think I'm right for this job," she told Nate and Kim. "I know something about jewelry, I'm a careful worker, and I'm very good at solving problems."

"I know you got good grades in school. That will be on your record," said Kim.

"The trouble is I haven't worked very much before," Jean said. "That might mean a lot to an interviewer."

"It could be a problem," said Nate, "but think about what a jewelry buyer does. Tell the interviewer you have learned to solve problems in your life, and you can do that on the job, too."

Instructor's Notes: Read the questions with students. Help students review and predict. Then have students read the story silently.

106

Unit 7

As they walked from the park, Jean couldn't stop thinking about her interview. She was set on a career as a jewelry buyer.

At Center Street, Kim stopped walking. "Hold it!" she yelled. She was looking at a big table. "This is my lucky day! Someone put this table out for pickup." Kim looked the center of the table over carefully. "It's not too clean," she said, "but that can be fixed. How old do you think it is?"

"Who knows?" said Nate. "It's a once-in-a-lifetime find!"

"Well, I need a table! Can you help me get this home?" asked Kim.

But Kim, Nate, and Jean couldn't carry the table. It was much too heavy.

"Keep trying!" cried Kim.

It was no use. "We've gone about one inch," said Nate. "This won't work."

Jean leaned on the table to think. "Listen!" she said. "Let's try this. Give me your skates, Nate." First, Jean put Nate's skates on two of the table legs. Then she put her own skates on the other two legs.

"Good thinking!" said Kim. "You solve problems well!"

The three friends set out again. But the table did not go straight.

Nate said, "The skates are too big for the table legs."

"I see that," said Jean. She sat down to think again. In no time, she jumped up. "Socks!" she said. "Our socks will make the skates fit better."

So Jean and Nate put their socks on the table legs. Jean was right. Now the table legs fit in the center of the skates. It was no problem to get the heavy table to Kim's.

When Jean went for her interview at the Summer Company, she was careful to listen as Mr. Teller told her about the job. She could tell that customers came first.

"Problems come up," said Mr. Teller. "A buyer may make a mistake about the jewelry she buys for our stores. The jewelry may be wrong, or the customers may not like it. Then the buyer has to do something so we don't lose money. Do you know how to solve problems like this? Have you done it on other jobs?"

Jean looked Mr. Teller straight in the eye. "I'm at the beginning of my career," she said, "but I am a good problem solver." And she told him the story of Kim's table.

Mr. Teller listened. When Jean was done, he laughed and said, "That is the best story! If you can solve problems like that every day, you've got the job."

And that is how Jean got a job as a buyer's helper and began her career.

Comprehension

Think About It

1. How did Jean feel about her job interview?
2. How did Nate and Kim help Jean prepare for the interview?
3. How did Jean solve Kim's problem?
4. Sum up what happened in the story.

Write About It

Describe a problem you have had and tell how you solved it.

Instructor's Notes: Help students read and answer the questions. Write About It can be used as a writing or discussion assignment.

108

Unit 7

 **Comprehension** # Drawing Conclusions

> A **conclusion** is an opinion you form after putting facts together. A conclusion is usually not stated in a story. You have to come up with it yourself by "reading between the lines".
>
> **Use these tips to draw a conclusion.**
> 1. Read the story or paragraph.
> 2. Keep the facts in mind. List them.
> 3. Think about what the facts say to you.
> 4. Draw a conclusion based on the facts and their meaning for you.

A. Read this paragraph.

When Fay was still in school, she had a chance to learn a new job and get paid for it. She got her pay at the end of the week if she did good work or not. Why should she do her best? Sometimes she was late for work. When school was over, and Fay needed daily work, she wasn't asked to stay at this job.

B. Find four facts and list them.

Fact 1 _____

Fact 2 _____

Fact 3 _____

Fact 4 _____

C. Which is the best conclusion to draw? Circle the number.

1. Fay did not do very well in school.

2. Fay had a bad life at home.

3. Fay wasn't a very responsible worker.

Instructor's Notes: Discuss the tips with students. Discuss what *reading between the lines* means. Then read the directions together.

Days and Months

The name of each day of the week and month of the year begins with a capital letter. You can also write the days and most of the months in a short form, or abbreviation. These abbreviations begin with a capital letter and end with a period.

January = Jan.   Sunday = Sun.

A. Read each word and its abbreviation. Write the abbreviations.

Sunday = Sun. _____   Monday = Mon. _____

Tuesday = Tues. _____   Wednesday = Wed. _____

Thursday = Thurs. _____   Friday = Fri. _____

Saturday = Sat. _____

B. Read each word and its abbreviation. Write the abbreviation.

January = Jan. _____   February = Feb. _____

March = Mar. _____   April = Apr. _____

May, June, July   August = Aug. _____

September = Sept. _____   October = Oct. _____

November = Nov. _____   December = Dec. _____

C. Read the paragraph. Underline the names of months and days.

It was a wet Tuesday in June when Walker first looked for a job. He went to the job center on Wednesday, Thursday, and Friday. At first he was told, "We don't have any jobs listed. Try again in July, August, or September." By Saturday and Sunday, Walker didn't feel very hopeful, but on Thursday, he went back and got lucky.

Instructor's Notes: Discuss the examples with students. Explain that an abbreviation is pronounced the same way as the complete word. For example, *Sun.* is read and said as *Sunday*. Read each set of directions with students. For B, note that *May, June,* and *July* have no short forms.

110

Unit 7

D. Draw a line to match each word with its abbreviation.

1. Saturday   Feb.

2. November   Aug.

3. April   Apr.

4. Tuesday   Tues.

5. February   Sat.

6. August   Nov.

E. Rewrite each sentence so it is correct.

1. Jean's interview is for a friday in september.

_____

2. Can Walker begin work on the first monday in january?

_____

3. In june people at the Better Rug Co. do not work on fridays.

_____

F. Write three of your own sentences about a job interview. Use the name of a day or month in each sentence.

1. _____

2. _____

3. _____

Instructor's Notes: Read each set of directions with students. For F, discuss the sentences students will write.

111

Unit 7

schedule   assignment   lunch   complaint

A. Read the words above. Then read the work schedule and assignments.

Summer Company						
Buyer's Helpers Schedule and Assignments						
	9:00–11:00 AM	11:00–NOON	NOON–1:00 PM	1:00–2:00 PM	2:00–4:00 PM	4:00–5:00 PM
Jean	In Store	At Jewelry Makers	At Jewelry Makers	LUNCH	Customer Complaints	Recordkeeping
Lucky	Customer Complaints	In Store	LUNCH	In Store	At Jewelry Makers	Recordkeeping
April	At Jewelry Makers	In Store	In Store	LUNCH	Recordkeeping	Customer Complaints
Matt	Customer Complaints	LUNCH	Recordkeeping	At Jewelry Makers	In Store	At Jewelry Makers

B. Read the questions and write the answers.

1. **a.** When do the buyer's helpers begin their work day?

   _____

   b. When do they end their day? _____

2. **a.** What does Jean do first? _____

   b. At what time does she take customer complaints?

   _____

3. How long do these workers have for lunch? _____

4. Who is at the jewelry maker's at 2:00 PM? _____

Instructor's Notes: Read the new words and each set of directions with students. Help them read the work schedule and answer the questions. Use the Unit 7 Review on page 113 to conclude the unit. Then assign *Reading for Today Workbook Four*, Unit 7. Use Blackline Master 8: Certificate of Completion from the *Instructor's Guide* to recognize students who successfully complete this book.

112

Unit 7

 *Unit 7 Review*

A. Write the word that best completes each sentence.

> keep center now solve career customers

1. Bill told Jean about the learning _____ .

2. Jean wanted a _____ as a jewelry buyer.

3. Jean works for the Summer Company _____ .

4. She helps the jewelry buyer learn about their _____ .

B. Write -ear or -eep to make new words. Write the word that fits best in each sentence.

y + _____ = _____ Bill has been at the center for a

_____ .

h + _____ = _____ Jean listened to _____ what Bill had to say.

n + _____ = _____ The Summer Company is

_____ Jean's home.

k + _____ = _____ Jean wants a job she can

_____ .

C. Draw lines to match the words and abbreviations.

1. Wednesday   Mar.

2. October   Thurs.

3. Sunday   Wed.

4. March   Sun.

5. Thursday   Oct.

A. Write the words that complete each sentence.

jewelry	costs	spends	could
less	silver	too	much

1. My roommate makes _____ .

2. She uses _____ and some gold, _____ .

3. She _____ a lot of time on it.

4. How _____ did you pay for that ring?

5. She _____ make one like it.

6. Her jewelry costs a lot _____ .

B. Write the word under the correct heading.

lovely	coupons	make	again
congress	luck	worked	puts

One-syllable words

1. _____

2. _____

3. _____

4. _____

Two-syllable words

1. _____

2. _____

3. _____

4. _____

C. Write the word that fits best in each sentence.

because	so	after	by

1. I like Jan _____ she is helpful.

2. She helps me _____ listening to my problems.

3. I feel better _____ a talk with Jan.

4. She has helped me, _____ I thank her.

D. Write the word that fits best in each sentence.

1. My mother _____ a radio to buy.
　　　　　　　　　find　found

2. The trouble was that she _____ too much for it.
　　　　　　　　　　　　　　　spent　spend

3. "This is _____ to be a used radio, Mom," I said.
　　　　　　likely　needy

4. She _____ the radio back to the store.
　　　　　took　take

5. Isn't it _____ that I looked at it?
　　　　　lucky　safely

E. Write the word that best completes each sentence.

late	know	small	report
always	means	where	after

1. I am responsible for making a _____ about our workday.

2. I _____ do it as well as I can.

3. It's not a _____ job, and it takes some time.

4. I _____ the boss looks at the report _____ work.

5. A good report _____ more pay for all of us.

F. Add -ink, -y, -eet, -ean, -ate, or -ock to make new words. Write the word that fits best in the sentence.

1. wh + _____ = _____   _____ is the baby crying?

2. l + _____ = _____   I am _____ with her food.

3. r + _____ = _____   Please _____ her while I get it.

4. th + _____ = _____   I _____ she likes that.

5. f + _____ = _____   She kicks her _____ .

G. Write the word that fits best in each sentence.

1. Will you _____ that tape for me?
         rerun   remind

2. It is _____ to me how it works.
        unclear   unlucky

3. _____ the tag on the tape.
      Undo   Unsold

4. Now _____ what it says.
        repay   reread

H. Add -s or -ies to the word for each sentence.

1. (family) Our _____ live far from us.

2. (party) We get together for big _____ now and then.

3. (try) My wife _____ to cook for all of us.

4. (stay) My brother _____ with us longer than anyone.

I. Write the words that fit best in each sentence.

customers	listen	careful	would
bring	thank	foreign	around

1. I work for a company that has many _____ .

2. Some customers use languages that are _____ to me.

3. I am _____ to listen to every word.

4. I _____ out the things the customers want.

5. I'm straight with my customers and I always _____ them.

6. Maybe you _____ like a job like this.

J. Add -ack, -ank, -ub, -ing, -ear, or -eep to make new words. Write the word that fits best in the sentence.

1. k + _____ = _____ I _____ some money in my wallet.

2. y + _____ = _____ Every _____ I save more.

3. b + _____ = _____ I put money in the _____ .

4. l + _____ = _____ I don't ever _____ food.

5. br + _____ = _____ I _____ food home.

K. Draw lines to match the words and abbreviations.

1. April   Dec.

2. avenue   Apr.

3. December   Dr.

4. doctor   Ave.

At Your Leisure

It Couldn't Be Done

Somebody said that it couldn't be done,
But he with a chuckle replied
That "maybe it couldn't," but he would be one
Who wouldn't say so till he'd tried.

So he buckled right in with the trace of a grin
On his face. If he worried he hid it.
He started to sing as he tackled the thing
That couldn't be done, and he did it.

by Edgar A. Guest

What About You?

Have you or someone you know ever overcome an obstacle to achieve a goal?

Overcoming Obstacles

Camara Barrett had more reason than most students to be nervous about taking a test to get into college. The New York City teenager was homeless. The shelters he visited were noisy, so Camara decided to find a nice, quiet place to study. After school, Camara went to the subway and boarded the No. 3 train. For four days and three nights, he studied on the train. He did so well on the test that he was accepted by eight colleges. He chose to attend one that offered him a full scholarship.

For a homeless teenager to finish high school and win a college scholarship is a great achievement. However, that is not all that Camara accomplished. Camara also found time to participate in his school community. He served as the editor of his school newspaper and student body president. In addition, Camara worked as a waiter and busboy in a Manhattan restaurant.

Many people have found Camara's story amazing. At the time, though, Camara wasn't thinking about impressing people. "I never thought I'd get all this attention," he says. "I didn't want publicity or money—I just wanted a scholarship because I knew I couldn't pay for college. . . ." Instead of thinking about the obstacles he faced, Camara focused on his goal. He knew that education would help him achieve the security he wanted. He didn't even think about the possibility of failing. "Failing would have meant losing out on all my ambitions," he said, "and I'd have ended up in the gutter somewhere, so I didn't think about it too much because it was too scary." He just went out and did what he needed to do.

Answer Key

Unit 1

Page 4

A. Answers will vary.

B. 1. Ben Nighthorse Campbell takes (action) in (many) (different) ways.

2. Campbell (still) (does) a job he learned as a (child).

3. He is good at (working) (together) with (different) (people).

4. Campbell (holds) down (more) than one job (because) he can do (many) things well.

C. 1. different   2. many

3. working

Page 5

B. 1. Ben Nighthorse Campbell is an <u>American Indian</u>.

2. He has <u>been</u> of help to people with problems.

3. Campbell works to make bills into <u>laws</u>.

4. <u>American Indians</u> want action on these <u>laws</u>.

5. There have <u>been</u> problems about the water rights of different groups <u>here</u>.

C. 1. here   2. American Indians

3. been   4. laws

D. The land and water in the United States are different from when <u>American Indians</u> lived on the land. People came to the United States to make homes <u>here</u> and took a lot of the land. They have used up or hurt the water in some way. Campbell has <u>been</u> working to make <u>laws</u> that fix these problems.

Page 6

B. 1. People <u>elected</u> Campbell because he is a man of action.

2. In the United States <u>senators</u> are <u>elected</u> to help make laws.

3. <u>Senator</u> Campbell owns and runs a <u>horse</u> <u>ranch</u> as well.

C. 1. elected   2. senator

3. ranch   4. horses

D. At his <u>ranch</u>, <u>Senator</u> Campbell can ride <u>horses</u> and work with his <u>ranch</u> hands. He doesn't have the time for his <u>ranch</u> that he used to, but he gets there when he can. He gives his job as <u>senator</u> his all because he was <u>elected</u> by the people.

Page 7

B. 1. Campbell learned how to make <u>jewelry</u> when he was a child.

2. Campbell's teacher in <u>jewelry</u> making was his father.

3. He sometimes <u>puts</u> stones in his <u>silver</u> jewelry.

4. People who like his work come to him for <u>jewelry</u> <u>again</u>.

C. 1. puts   2. silver

3. again   4. jewelry

D. Will Campbell find time to make more <u>silver</u> jewelry? He says he won't give up doing work he likes this well. He works on the <u>silver</u> jewelry at night. That way he can go to his job as senator <u>again</u> in the daytime and still <u>put</u> in time making <u>silver</u> jewelry.

Page 8

B.

One Syllable	Two Syllables
1. law	**1.** problem
2. more	**2.** rancher
3. group	**3.** safety
4. own	**4.** father
5. like	**5.** country

C.
1. <u>Ben</u> <u>Campbell</u> <u>holds</u> <u>down</u> <u>many</u> jobs.
2. <u>Campbell</u> <u>owns</u> <u>a</u> <u>horse</u> <u>ranch</u>.
3. <u>Sometimes</u> <u>he</u> <u>works</u> <u>with</u> <u>silver</u>.
4. <u>He</u> <u>puts</u> <u>in</u> <u>time</u> <u>working</u> <u>for</u> <u>people</u>.

Page 9

B.

wallet—2	different—3	someone—2
plan—1	learned—1	uniform—3
value—2	street—1	video—3

D.

again—a	doctor—o	parent—e
holiday—i	problem—e	person—o

Page 12

<u>Think About It</u>

Discuss your answers with your instructor.

1. He works to get action taken on problems. He knows how to do many things well and knows how to talk to people.

2. Answers will vary. Possible answers include helping make laws, talking to people about problems, serving on groups or committees in the Senate.

3. He makes silver jewelry and raises horses.

4. Summaries should include his many activities as senator, craftsman, and rancher, as well as his interest in the world at large and people in general.

<u>Write About It</u>

Discuss your writing with your instructor.

Page 13

A. 3

B. 1

C. <u>Since Campbell is an American Indian,</u> (he took the name Ben Nighthorse.)

Page 14

A.

1. differently	**1.** needy
2. lovely	**2.** handy
3. safely	**3.** hilly
4. likely	**4.** lucky
5. nightly	**5.** mighty

B. Campbell does things <u>differently</u>. He holds down more than one job, and he works for <u>needy</u> causes. The people are <u>lucky</u> that they elected him senator. His <u>friendly</u> ways are <u>likely</u> to get him elected again.

C.
1. nightly
2. lovely
3. handy

Page 15

D.
1. lucky
2. friendly
3. finely
4. handy
5. healthy
6. hilly

E.
1. differently
2. likely
3. lucky
4. safely

F. Discuss your sentences with your instructor.

B. **1.** b **2.** c **3.** a

C. Discuss your letter with your instructor.

Unit 1 Review

Page 17

A. **1.** elected **2.** horse ranch *or* ranch, jewelry

3. American Indian **4.** senator

B. **1.** make **1.** lovely

2. luck **2.** letter

3. worked **3.** silver

4. puts **4.** congress

C. **1.** lovely **2.** nightly **3.** needy

Unit 2

Page 20

A. Answers will vary.

B. **1.** (Buyers) like Kay (want) all the (things) they (see).

2. Do they buy (because) they (need) all (these) (things)?

3. Kay doesn't (need) (many) of the (things) she buys.

4. Store owners can make money when they (sell) to (buyers) like Kay.

C. **1.** baseball **2.** seven

3. game

Page 21

B. **1.** I read the ads and <u>then</u> clip out the <u>coupons</u>.

2. Do I need to <u>save</u> all the <u>coupons</u> I see?

3. <u>Could</u> they help me <u>save</u> on something I need?

4. I <u>could</u> clip out the <u>coupons</u> I want to use.

5. <u>Then</u> I <u>could</u> use the <u>coupons</u> to get the things I need.

C. **1.** could **2.** coupons

3. then **4.** save

D. Nan and Kay want to <u>save</u> money when they shop. One way they <u>could</u> <u>save</u> money is to use <u>coupons</u>. Nan finds <u>coupons</u> in the store ads, and <u>then</u> Kay clips out the ones that <u>could</u> help them <u>save</u>. They <u>save</u> a lot of <u>coupons</u> and <u>then</u> buy the things they need.

Page 22

B. **1.** Many people could pay <u>less</u> using coupons, but they don't <u>think</u> about it.

2. The right way to use coupons is to <u>think</u> about what you are buying.

3. How <u>much</u> money does meat <u>cost</u> without the coupon?

4. Will meat <u>cost</u> more or <u>less</u> at a different store?

C. **1.** less **2.** think

3. much **4.** cost

D. Food <u>costs</u> more and more these days. I <u>think</u> we could save money by using coupons. But we have to <u>think</u> about some things when we shop. How <u>much</u> does food <u>cost</u> when we use coupons? Will the <u>cost</u> be <u>less</u> at a big store that has a lot of goods? How <u>much</u> trouble is it to get to that store?

Page 23

B. **1.** My <u>roommate</u> saves all the coupons she sees.

2. Then she <u>spends</u> money for things we don't need.

3. When we shop together, she doesn't buy <u>too</u> much.

4. <u>Why</u> can't she do that when I'm not with her?

5. I think my <u>roommate</u> could learn to stop buying things we don't need.

C. **1.** Why   **2.** too

     3. roommate   **4.** spend

D. My <u>roommate</u> has a problem when she goes shopping without me. She <u>spends</u> money on things we don't need because she thinks she saves money. Then we have <u>too</u> many things, but not what we need. <u>Why</u> do store ads and coupons make people want things they can't use? I'm going to help my <u>roommate</u> quit buying things we don't need.

Page 24

A.

<u>br</u>and	<u>cr</u>eam	<u>dr</u>ive	<u>fr</u>iend
<u>br</u>ag	<u>cr</u>op	<u>dr</u>op	<u>fr</u>om
<u>gr</u>oup	<u>pr</u>oblem	<u>tr</u>ouble	<u>str</u>eet
<u>gr</u>ay	<u>pr</u>ison	<u>tr</u>uck	<u>str</u>ap

B.

gray	drip
fray	grip
tray	strip
stray	trip

C. **1.** brag   **2.** trip

     3. brand   **4.** tray

Page 25

A. cry, dry, fry, try

B. **1.** my   **2.** try

     3. why

C. wink, brink, drink

D. **1.** drink   **2.** drink

     3. think

Page 28

<u>Think About It</u>

Discuss your answers with your instructor.

1. They wanted to get enough coupons from the packages to send them in and win tickets to a baseball game.

2. They won more hot dogs.

3. She found out that using coupons doesn't always save money. She learned that she sometimes bought something she didn't really need just because she had a coupon.

4. Summaries should include the fact that the roommates have different ideas about using coupons. Kay buys whatever she has coupons for and Nan thinks she shouldn't do that. Nan tries her own way of using coupons, but her plan doesn't work either. The roommates learn they need to think about which coupons they can use.

<u>Write About It</u>

Discuss your writing with your instructor.

Page 29

B. Fact 1: Matt looked at the coupons.

Fact 2: They were for tea bags.

Fact 3: Matt gave the coupons to Kay.

Fact 4: She used them when she went to the store.

C. **3.** Kay likes tea.

Page 30

B. I <u>gave</u> some coupons to my roommate, and she <u>took</u> them to the store. Kay <u>thought</u> all the coupons <u>were</u> good, and she <u>bought</u> a lot of things. Then she <u>found</u> out the coupons <u>were</u> good in May, but not in June. I hope this <u>taught</u> Kay to read coupons well.

C. **1.** sold   **2.** paid

123

Page 31

D. 1. spent   2. taught

     3. were   4. began

     5. took

E. 1. find   2. Give

     3. buy   4. pay

F. Discuss your sentences with your instructor.

Page 32

B. 1. coupon 1   2. ounce

     3. coupon 1, 50¢; coupon 2, 25¢

Unit 2 Review

Page 33

A. 1. coupons   2. could

     3. roommate   4. think

B. 1. why; why   2. drink, dry; drink

     3. try; try   4. think; think

C. 1. sold   2. paid

     3. made, spent

Unit 3

Page 36

A. Answers will vary.

B. 1. Will Jay be (upset) because I can't (teach) him to read?

     2. I (gave) him help with baseball, but (who) will be his reading (teacher)?

     3. When Jay (takes) time with his work, he does not get (into) trouble.

     4. We'll all work (together) to help Jay (learn) to read.

C. 1. b   2. c

     3. a

Page 37

B. 1. Mr. Sanders <u>always</u> wanted to go to <u>school</u>.

     2. Going to <u>school</u> <u>means</u> you have a chance to learn.

     3. <u>Schools</u> are not <u>always</u> for children.

     4. A teacher <u>must</u> spend a lot of time helping people learn.

     5. Does our teacher <u>mean</u> that we <u>must</u> <u>always</u> do well?

C. 1. school   2. always

     3. must   4. mean

D. Some parents think <u>schools</u> <u>must</u> <u>always</u> teach children to read. But children <u>must</u> get help at home with the things they learn at <u>school</u>. What does this <u>mean</u> for parents who can't read well? Sometimes these parents <u>must</u> get help, too.

Page 38

B. 1. Mr. Sanders must <u>meet</u> his son's teacher <u>soon</u>.

     2. Jay told his father <u>where</u> to find the teacher.

     3. Mrs. Keating said she will <u>meet</u> Mr. Sanders.

     4. <u>Soon</u> he will talk to her about Jay's problem.

     5. <u>After</u> this talk, Mr. Sanders will help Jay.

C. 1. after   2. meet

     3. soon   4. Where

D. Parents may have problems to work out when they <u>meet</u> with a teacher. They must find out <u>where</u> the school is. Sometimes both the child and parents must find a time to <u>meet</u> together with the teacher. Parents might need to be at home <u>soon</u> <u>after</u> work. But when parents and teachers find time for these <u>meetings</u>, they can work out ways to help a child.

Page 39

B. **1.** In school you may have to give a <u>report</u>.

2. Will you get a good <u>or</u> bad <u>grade</u>?

3. A <u>report</u> that makes the reader think will get a good <u>grade</u>.

4. Children don't get good <u>grades</u> on <u>report cards</u> because they are lucky.

5. Good <u>grades</u> mean the child did good work.

C. **1.** report   **2.** grade

3. card   **4.** or

D. What does a good <u>grade</u> on a <u>report</u> <u>card</u> mean? It means the child did a lot of work to get the <u>grade</u>. Some children have trouble giving a <u>report</u>. A parent can help by talking with the child about what to say in the <u>report</u>, <u>or</u> they can spend time reading it together. Soon the child will get good <u>grades</u> on <u>report</u> <u>cards</u>.

Page 40

A. <u>sc</u>an   <u>sk</u>in   <u>sl</u>ip   <u>sm</u>oke

<u>sc</u>old   <u>sk</u>y   <u>sl</u>ed   <u>sm</u>ell

snip   <u>sp</u>end   <u>st</u>and   <u>sw</u>im

<u>sn</u>ake   <u>sp</u>ell   <u>st</u>ore   <u>sw</u>ay

B. slay   sky

stay   sly

sway   spy

C. **1.** spell   **2.** stay

3. slip   **4.** spend

5. stand

Page 41

A. greet, sleet, sweet

B. **1.** meet   **2.** sweet

3. greet

C. Dean, Jean, wean

D. **1.** Jean   **2.** mean

3. lean

Page 44

<u>Think About It</u>

Discuss your answers with your instructor.

1. He got a job and quit school.

2. He wants to help his son with his school work.

3. She suggests that he attend reading classes for adults at the school.

4. Summaries should include the idea that Jay's trouble with reading and spelling made Mr. Sanders realize how much he needed to learn to read so he can help his son. Mr. Sanders talks to Jay's teacher and finds out it's not too late to go back to school.

<u>Write About It</u>

Discuss your writing with your instructor.

Page 45

A. **1.** b   **2.** c

3. b

B. Parents Are Teachers, Too

Page 46

A. **1.** reread   **1.** unlucky

2. remind   **2.** unsold

3. repay   **3.** unclear

4. rerun   **4.** unloved

B. Jay thinks he is <u>unlucky</u> to have a teacher who makes him work a lot. But someday he will want to <u>repay</u> her for her help. The teacher tells Jay that he must <u>reread</u> things many times. She makes him <u>redo</u> work that has mistakes in it.

C. **1.** unclear **2.** remind

3. undo **4.** unloved

Page 47

D. **1.** rethink

2. reteach

3. repaid

4. retell

1. undone

2. unsaid

3. unsafe

4. unhurt

E. **1.** rerun

2. unplanned

3. unhurt

4. unsold

5. unsaid

6. reteach

7. retell

8. rethink

F. Discuss your sentences with your instructor.

Page 48

B. **1.** Jay made his best grade in math.

2. Jay's worst grade was an F. He got an F in both reading and spelling.

3. No, Jay doesn't do his work on time. He got an Unsatisfactory on the part of his report card for "Turns work in on time." That's probably part of the reason he got low grades in reading and spelling.

Unit 3 Review

Page 49

A. **1.** always **2.** grades

3. means **4.** must, after

B. **1.** meet, mean; meet **2.** greet; greet

3. Jean; Jean **4.** meet, mean; mean

C. **1.** unclear **2.** reread

3. remind **4.** unlucky

Unit 4

Page 52

A. Answers will vary.

B. **1.** I gave Maria a ⟨hug⟩ when I learned about our ⟨child⟩.

2. The ⟨doctor⟩ at the ⟨clinic⟩ said our ⟨child⟩ will ⟨come⟩ in June.

3. I'm a ⟨heavy⟩ ⟨smoker⟩, but I ⟨hope⟩ to quit soon for our ⟨child's⟩ sake.

C.

	¹u		²d			³s	
⁴p	a	r	e	n	t	s	
			i			r	
			v			e	
			e			e	
						t	

Page 53

B. **1.** My <u>wife</u> Maria is doing what the doctor told her.

2. We're learning how to be <u>responsible</u> parents.

3. My <u>wife</u> stopped smoking because it isn't good for the <u>baby</u>.

4. <u>As</u> a mother-to-be, she must think of her health.

5. <u>Responsible</u> parents try to make a good life for their children.

C. **1.** wife   **2.** baby

    3. responsible   **4.** as, as

D. After my <u>wife</u> found out she was going to have a <u>baby</u>, we both stopped smoking. We're <u>responsible</u> for our <u>baby's</u> health. <u>As</u> our child gets big, we'll feel <u>responsible</u> for the child's schooling <u>as</u> well.

Page 54

B. **1.** <u>Before</u> you <u>know</u> it, we'll have a <u>new</u> baby.

    2. Do you think the baby will <u>know</u> that I'm a <u>new</u> father?

    3. To be a good father, I must learn many <u>new</u> things.

    4. I need to <u>know</u> how to carry a <u>small</u> child.

    5. What do <u>new</u> parents feed a <u>small</u> baby?

C. **1.** Before   **2.** new

    3. know   **4.** Small

D. We have a lot to think about <u>before</u> the baby comes. My wife and I will be responsible for a <u>new</u> life. Does a <u>small</u> child cry all night? Will I need to spend more time at home than I did <u>before</u>? We <u>know</u> our lives are going to be different, but we feel good about a <u>new</u> baby in the family.

Page 55

B. **1.** Maria's best friend Jan is <u>pregnant</u>, too.

    2. Jan tells Maria that all <u>pregnant</u> women don't feel <u>tired</u>.

    3. She <u>rocks</u> the baby to stop it from crying.

    4. Jan says that new parents may feel <u>tired</u> from getting up <u>late</u> at night to feed the baby.

C. **1.** late   **2.** rock

    3. tired   **4.** pregnant

D. Maria was feeling <u>tired</u>, and she went to see the doctor. That was when she found out she is <u>pregnant</u>. I came home <u>late</u> that night, but she was up to tell me the good news. As soon as the baby comes, I want to spend time <u>rocking</u> our baby.

Page 56

A. <u>bl</u>end   <u>cl</u>inic   <u>fl</u>y

    <u>bl</u>ink   <u>cl</u>an   <u>fl</u>ag

    <u>gl</u>ad   <u>pl</u>ayer   <u>sl</u>y

    <u>gl</u>and   <u>pl</u>an   <u>sl</u>eet

B. blink   blight

    clink   flight

    plink   plight

    slink   slight

C. **1.** plan   **2.** plight

    3. glad

Page 57

A. block, clock, smock

B. **1.** rock   **2.** smock

    3. clock   **4.** block *or* blocks

C. plate, skate, state

D. **1.** late   **2.** date

    3. plate   **4.** rate

Page 60

<u>Think About It</u>

Discuss your answers with your instructor.

1. Yes. They feel lucky, have told their families, have prepared for the baby's arrival, and have made changes in their own lives (stopped smoking).

2. They will have to rearrange their schedules to see that the baby's needs are met. They may be tired from getting up at night when the baby cries.

3. They'll feed and rock the child and see that the child gets a good education.

4. Summaries should include the idea that Maria and Carlos have done a lot of thinking and planning that will make having a new baby easier to take care of. They are both happy that they are having a child and look forward to being responsible parents.

<u>Write About It</u>

Discuss your writing with your instructor.

Page 61

B. 1. Carlos and Maria will be responsible parents.

C. Responsible Parents

Page 62

A. 1. families   2. cries
   3. cities   4. tries
   5. babies   6. countries

B. <u>countries</u>, <u>cities</u>, <u>families</u>

C. 1. families   2. cries
   3. tries   4. babies
   5. countries

Page 63

D. 1. keys   2. stays
   3. toys   4. pays
   5. days   6. plays

E. 1. families   2. stays
   3. toys   4. boys
   5. plays   6. tries

F. Discuss your sentences with your instructor.

Page 64

B. 1. Maria should take one tablet daily.

2. Maria should call the drugstore or pharmacy to get more tablets.

3. There are 100 tablets in the bottle. There is 100 beside Qty., or quantity.

4. No, Maria's father should not take the tablets. These tablets may not help him with his problem. He should see his own doctor.

Unit 4 Review

Page 65

A. 1. wife   2. responsible
   3. Before   4. new

B. 1. plate; plate   2. block; block
   3. late, lock; late   4. rate, rock; rock

C. 1. families   2. cries
   3. babies

Unit 5

Page 68

A. Answers will vary.

B. 1. One (day), Jack and (Kate) (took) the kids to the lake in their (truck).

2. They had a (bag) of (food), a (tape) (player), and a (camera).

3. We are not all the (same), but Jack doesn't like people who are (different) from (him).

C. **1.** c   **2.** b   **3.** a   **4.** d

Page 69

B. **1.** Some friends of mine went to a <u>foreign</u> country this <u>summer</u>.

2. They did not know how to get <u>around</u> and had trouble talking to the people there.

3. As soon as they could get <u>around</u>, my friends <u>saw</u> a lot of the city.

C. **1.** Summer   **2.** foreign

3. saw   **4.** around

D. When my family came to this country, it was a <u>foreign</u> land to them. They did not know how to get <u>around</u> in a big city. They were not used to the hot <u>summers</u>. Things were different for them, but they <u>saw</u> this <u>foreign</u> land as a chance for a new life.

Page 70

B. **1.** We ate different <u>snacks</u> at our <u>picnic</u>.

2. <u>Thank</u> you, Mom, for all these <u>snacks</u>.

3. The bugs at the <u>park</u> liked our <u>picnic</u>, too.

4. After all, what is a <u>park</u> <u>picnic</u> without a bug or two?

C. **1.** picnic   **2.** snacks

3. thank   **4.** park

D. This summer we had a family <u>picnic</u> in the <u>park</u>. The sun was out all day, and the food was good. We ate <u>snacks</u>, played baseball, and talked. My mother made all the food for the <u>picnic</u>. Did we <u>thank</u> her for all these <u>snacks</u>?

Page 71

B. **1.** Many <u>newcomers</u> go to the park in the summer.

2. Some of them use a different <u>language</u>.

3. All the children run and <u>jump</u> in the <u>grass</u> together.

4. The <u>newcomers</u> sit at a table by Jack and his family.

C. **1.** newcomers   **2.** language

3. jump   **4.** grass

D. People in the park may use different foreign <u>languages</u>. But they all like picnics and a swim in the lake. All the children like to run in the <u>grass</u> and <u>jump</u> into the cold water. <u>Language</u> isn't a problem for them. Reed, Nell, and the <u>newcomers</u> just yell and <u>jump</u> and have fun.

Page 72

A. <u>ch</u>ance   <u>sh</u>y   <u>shr</u>ug
<u>ch</u>ild   <u>sh</u>ake   <u>shr</u>ink
<u>th</u>en   <u>th</u>ank   <u>wh</u>en
<u>th</u>at   <u>th</u>ing   <u>wh</u>y

B. chin   shine
shin   shrine
thin   whine

C. **1.** shine   **2.** that

3. chin   **4.** whine

5. thank

Page 73

A. black, shack, stack, track

B. **1.** pack   **2.** sack

3. black   **4.** back

C. blank, drank, frank

D. **1.** bank   **2.** drank

3. sank

Page 76

<u>Think About It</u>

1. He doesn't like them.

2. Jack thinks the man hurt his son Reed.

3. Jack does change his mind because he thanks the newcomer and shakes hands with him.

4. Summaries should include that the Bakers went to the park for a picnic, as they had done before. When they arrived, some different-looking people were there, and Jack, the father, didn't like it. The children all played together. Then Jack's son cut his hand and the other father helped him. Jack was angry at first, but eventually he realized that these people were not so different after all.

<u>Write About It</u>

Discuss your writing with your instructor.

Page 77

A. 3, 2, 1

B. **1.** b   **2.** a

Page 78

A. 1. stillness   1. thankful

   2. neatness   2. playful

   3. sadness   3. useful

   4. sickness   4. handful

   5. shyness   5. hopeful

B. I'm <u>hopeful</u> that we'll have a good day for our picnic. The children will be <u>playful</u> in the park. I've told them to be <u>helpful</u> when we get there. I'm glad that <u>sickness</u> didn't keep the family at home.

C. **1.** handful   **2.** shyness

   3. thankful

Page 79

D. The newcomer tried to be <u>useful</u>. He showed <u>sadness</u> when Jack yelled at him. But now Jack and the newcomer feel <u>hopeful</u> about one another.

E. **1.** neatness   **2.** playful

   3. handful   **4.** stillness

F. **1.** hopeful   **2.** thankful

   3. shyness

Page 80

B. **1.** Yes, most parks have rules like these to make the park safe for visitors and to protect the park grounds.

   2. Rules 1–4 are specifically addressed to safety issues. Students may also agree that Rules 5 and 6 pertain to safety, too.

   3. Rules 4 and 6

   4. Answers will vary. Students might mention rules about alcohol, loud music, use of boats on the lake, fishing rules.

Unit 5 Review

Page 81

A. **1.** park *or* picnic   **2.** newcomers

   3. foreign   **4.** jump

B. **1.** pack; pack   **2.** back *or* bank, back

   3. thank; thank   **4.** bank *or* back, bank

C. **1.** thankful   **2.** goodness

   3. helpful

Unit 6

Page 84

A. Answers will vary.

B. 1. (Sometimes) I have (problems) talking to a (person) I don't know.

2. My (own) (wife) tells me I can be a (fine) (talker) but it (does) not help me.

3. Being in a big group (gives) me a (lonely) feeling.

C.

¹c	a	r	²r	y
			o	
³t	a	l	k	e	r
			d	

Page 85

B. 1. I <u>would</u> like to be a <u>better</u> talker.

2. Who can I <u>ask</u> to help me get <u>over</u> this problem?

3. I can <u>ask</u> my friend Fran to help me.

4. I could not <u>ask</u> for a <u>better</u> friend than Fran.

C. 1. would   2. ask

3. better   4. over

D. <u>Would</u> you feel lonely in a big group of people? I <u>would</u>. Fran says I'd <u>better</u> learn to talk. <u>Over</u> and <u>over</u> again she tells me this, "Walk around and soon you'll meet a person who <u>would</u> like to chat."

Page 86

B. 1. My wife likes to go to <u>every</u> <u>party</u>, big or small.

2. I <u>never</u> want to go to a <u>party</u> where there are lots of people.

3. When I meet new people, I <u>never</u> know what to say.

4. I always feel better when I can <u>bring</u> my wife.

5. For a shy person like me, <u>every</u> <u>party</u> is lonely.

C. 1. never   2. every

3. party   4. bring

D. When I'm at a big <u>party</u>, I would like to feel better than I do. <u>Every</u> other person seems to be having a good time, but I'm faking it. Being around people I don't know <u>brings</u> out my shyness. I <u>never</u> know the right thing to say. Does a big <u>party</u> make you feel this way?

Page 87

B. 1. My wife's <u>company</u> gives a big party on a holiday.

2. She always asks me to <u>join</u> her friends from work.

3. They talk about people and things from the <u>company</u>.

4. Because I don't know what they are talking about, I feel that I don't <u>belong</u> there.

5. I must learn how to <u>join</u> the <u>club</u>.

C. 1. company   2. belong

3. club   4. join

D. When my wife's <u>company</u> gives a party, I don't have a good time. I feel like I'm on my own, that I don't <u>belong</u> to the group. I don't know how to <u>join</u> in the fun. Why do I feel that they have a <u>club</u> and I don't <u>belong</u> to it?

Page 88

A. <u>write</u>   <u>know</u>   g<u>ui</u>tar   ri<u>gh</u>t

     <u>wr</u>ap   <u>kn</u>it   g<u>ui</u>de   <u>kn</u>i<u>gh</u>t

B.   knit   wrote

     knock   wring

     knot   wry

     knight   wrap

     knee   wren

C.   **1.** know   **2.** wring

     3. knit   **4.** wrap

     5. right

Page 89

A. spring, string, swing, wring

B.   **1.** swing   **2.** sing

     3. bring

C. grub, shrub, snub

D.   **1.** club   **2.** snub

     3. hub

Page 92

Think About It

Discuss your answers with your instructor.

1. He feels shy and uncomfortable, not at ease with people he doesn't know.

2. She is outgoing and at ease in social situations. She talks and laughs with others.

3. She suggests ways he can start a conversation, and ways he can enjoy himself, like playing the guitar or getting people involved in games.

4. Summaries should include the idea that Rick dislikes parties because he is shy, but that after talking with Fran he feels he might be able to overcome his shyness.

Write About It

Discuss your writing with your instructor.

Page 93

A.   **1.** No   **2.** Yes

B.   **1.** shy   **2.** like

Page 94

A. St., Dr., oz., g, Rd., Ave., lb., km

B. My wife works for the Clay <u>Co</u>. on Shell <u>Ave</u>. The company has a health plan with <u>Dr</u>. Parker. The doctor works at Pope <u>St</u>. and School <u>Rd</u>. I will see <u>Dr</u>. Parker at the company party on Sunday, June 4.

C.   **1.** road   **2.** doctor

     3. company   **4.** mister

     5. avenue

Page 95

D.   **1.** 24 Spring St.   **2.** Dr. and Mrs. Gates

     3. the Silver Ranch   **4.** 1 lb. and 2 oz.
     Co.

E.   **1.** Dr. Key   **2.** Land Ave.

     3. 25 g   **4.** Dean Co.

     5. Dune St.   **6.** 5 km

     7. Waters Rd.

F. Discuss your sentences with your instructor.

Page 96

B.   **1.** Sentences 2 and 4 tell you what not to do if you are feeling shy.

     2. Answers will vary.

     3. Many people are shy. There may be other people who are feeling the same way you are.

Unit 6 Review

Page 97

A. 1. never   2. would

     3. belong   4. Every

B. 1. club, cling; club   2. snub; snub

     3. swing; swing   4. bring; bring

C. 1. St.   2. km

     3. Ave.   4. oz.

     5. Dr.

Unit 7

Page 100

A. Answers will vary.

B. 1. I would like to (learn) a (responsible) job and (join) a big (company).

     2. I know I need to look (right) (when) I go to a meeting (about) a (new) job.

     3. I'll make a (list) of what I (should) do.

     4. I don't (want) (problems) (when) I go to this meeting.

C. 1. join   2. learn

     3. new   4. problems

     5. right   6. want

Page 101

B. 1. Jean's school runs a job <u>center</u>.

     2. Bill has worked at the <u>center</u> for a <u>year</u>.

     3. He <u>keeps</u> telling Jean about new jobs.

     4. <u>Now</u> she is going to talk to someone about a job.

C. 1. year   2. Now

     3. center   4. keep

D. Jean went to the <u>center</u> at the end of the school <u>year</u>. "<u>Now</u> is the time to get a job," she said. Jean wanted a responsible job that she could <u>keep</u> for many <u>years</u>. She talked to people at the <u>center</u> about what she could do. Jean will <u>keep</u> looking if this job doesn't work out.

Page 102

B. 1. Jean <u>once</u> had a job at a store.

     2. Her <u>interview</u> is for a different job.

     3. In this job she would have to <u>solve</u> many problems.

     4. You need to <u>listen</u> to people to <u>solve</u> problems.

C. 1. once   2. listen

     3. solve   4. interview

D. Jean didn't know what an <u>interview</u> was like. "We can <u>solve</u> that," said Bill. "I'll help you with this upcoming <u>interview</u>." They went over things <u>once</u> and then <u>once</u> more. "<u>Listen</u> to what the person says," Bill told Jean. "And talk so he or she <u>listens</u> to you."

Page 103

B. 1. Jean wants to begin a <u>career</u> as a buyer.

     2. She knows that she should be <u>careful</u> about how she looks.

     3. Standing up <u>straight</u> will make her look better.

     4. In this job Jean would have to know the company's <u>customers</u>.

C. 1. straight   2. customers

     3. careful   4. career

D. Where does a store get the things it sells to <u>customers</u>? A store has people called buyers who buy <u>straight</u> from the companies that make things. Jean wants a <u>career</u> at the Summer Company. At first she would help the jewelry buyer there. A buyer has to be very <u>careful</u>. If she buys the wrong things, <u>customers</u> might not like them.

Page 104

A. 1. wh(y)   1. bab(y)

2. m(y)   2. jewelr(y)

3. sh(y)   3. part(y)

4. dr(y)   4. lonel(y)

B. 1. sly   1. lucky

2. try   2. healthy

3. cry   3. many

4. fly   4. heavy

C. I've had <u>many</u> jobs over the years. I'm <u>lucky</u> to have a chance to (try) a new company. (My) old job didn't work for me, but I know (why.) Now I can interview for a good career and make <u>money</u> at the same time.

Page 105

A. sheep, sleep, steep, sweep

B. 1. keep   2. steep   3. sleep

C. clear, shear, smear, spear

D. 1. near   2. hear   3. clear

Page 108

<u>Think About It</u>

Discuss answers with students.

1. She was nervous about it because she didn't have much work experience.

2. They made suggestions about what to wear; they gave her moral support.

3. She suggested that they use their skates to wheel the table to Kim's house.

4. Summaries should include Jean's goal of a new job. Nate and Kim gave her suggestions about the interview. Moving the heavy table on rollerblades to Kim's home helped prove Jean was a good problem solver, a skill she needed for her new job.

<u>Write About It</u>

Discuss your writing with your instructor.

Page 109

B. 1. Fay was in training for a new job.

2. Fay got paid if she did good work or not.

3. She was sometimes late for work.

4. She was not asked to stay on as a full time employee when she got out of school.

C. 3

Page 110

A. Sun., Mon., Tues., Wed., Thurs., Fri., Sat.

B. Jan., Feb., Mar., Apr., Aug., Sept., Oct., Nov., Dec.

C. It was a wet <u>Tuesday</u> in <u>June</u> when Walker first looked for a job. He went to the job center on <u>Wednesday</u>, <u>Thursday</u>, and <u>Friday</u>. At first he was told, "We don't have any jobs listed. Try again in <u>July</u>, <u>August</u>, or <u>September</u>." By <u>Saturday</u> and <u>Sunday</u>, Walker didn't feel very hopeful, but on <u>Thursday</u>, he went back and got lucky.

Page 111

D. **1.** Sat.   **2.** Nov.

    3. Apr.   **4.** Tues.

    5. Feb.   **6.** Aug.

E. **1.** Jean's interview is for a Friday in September.

    2. Can Walker begin work on the first Monday in January?

    3. In June people at the Better Rug Company do not work on Fridays.

F. Discuss your sentences with your instructor.

Page 112

B. **1.** a. 9:00 A.M.

      b. 5:00 P.M.

    2. a. works in the store

      b. 2:00–4:00 P.M.

    3. one hour

    4. Matt *or* Lucky

Unit 7 Review

Page 113

A. **1.** center   **2.** career

    3. now   **4.** customers

B. **1.** year; year   **2.** hear; hear

    3. near; near   **4.** keep; keep

C. **1.** Wed.   **2.** Oct.

    3. Sun.   **4.** Mar.

    5. Thurs.

Final Review

Page 114

A. **1.** jewelry   **2.** silver, too

    3. spends   **4.** much

    5. could   **6.** less

B. One-syllable words:

make

luck

worked

puts

Two-syllable words:

lovely

coupons

again

congress

C. **1.** because   **2.** by

Page 115

    3. after   **4.** so

D. **1.** found   **2.** spent

    3. likely   **4.** took

    5. lucky

E. **1.** report   **2.** always

    3. small   **4.** know, after

    5. means

Page 116

F. **1.** y; why; Why

    2. ate, ink, ean, *or* ock; late, link, lean, *or* lock; late

    3. ock, ink, *or* ate; rock, rink, *or* rate; rock

    4. ink; think; think

    5. eet *or* ate; feet *or* fate; feet

G. **1.** rerun   **2.** unclear

     3. Undo   **4.** reread

H. **1.** families   **2.** parties

     3. tries   **4.** stays

Page 117

I. **1.** customers   **2.** foreign

     3. careful   **4.** bring

     5. thank   **6.** would

J. **1.** eep *or* ing; keep *or* king; keep

     2. ear *or* ank; year *or* yank; year

     3. ank *or* ack; bank *or* back; bank

     4. ack *or* ank; lack *or* lank; lack

     5. ing; bring; bring

K. **1.** Apr.   **2.** Ave.

     3. Dec.   **4.** Dr.

Word List

Below is a list of the 350 words that are presented to students in *Book Four* of *Reading for Today*. These words are introduced on sight word, phonics, comprehension, writing skills and life skills pages. The words will be reviewed in later books. Students should also be familiar with other words based on the phonetically regular spellings of long and short vowel sounds in the consonant-vowel-consonant (CVC) and consonant-vowel-consonant + silent *e* (CVC + *e*) patterns.

A
after
again
ago
always
Apr.
April
around
as
ask
assignment
attention
Aug.
August
Ave.
avenue

B
babies
baby
back
bank
bashful
bean
been
beet
before
began
begin
belong
best
better
black
blank
blend
blight

blink
block
bottle
bought
brag
brand
bring
brink

C
card
career
careful
center
chin
cities
clan
clean
clear
clink
clock
club
Co.
company
complaint
Congress
cost
could
countries
coupon
cream
cries
crop
cry
customer

D
daily
date
Dean
dear
Dec.
December
deep
differently
Dr.
drank
drink
drip
drop
drug
dry

E
elected
enjoy
every
expiration

F
families
fear
Feb.
February
feet
first
flag
flight
fly
foreign
found
fray

Fri.
Friday
friendly
fry

G
gate
glad
gland
goodness
government
grade
grass
gray
greet
grip
grub
guide

H
handful
handy
healthy
hear
helpful
here
hilly
hopeful
horse
hub

I
interview
invite

J
Jan.

January
Jean
jeep
jewelry
join
July
jump

K
keep
king
knee
knight
knit
knock
knot
know

L
language
late
law
lb.
lean
learned
less
letter
lifeguard
likely
list
listen
lock
longer
lovely
lunch

M
Mar.
March
math
May
mean
meet
mighty
mock
Mon.
Monday
most
much
must

N
name
Native
  American
near
neatness
needy
never
new
newcomers
nightly
Nov.
November
now

O
Oct.
October
once
or
other

137

ounce
over
owner
oz.

P

pack
paid
park
party
picnic
pink
plan
plate
playful
plight
plink
pound
pregnant
put

R

ranch
rancher
rate
Rd.
redo
relax
remember
remind
repay
report
reread
rerun
responsible
ring
rink
rock
roommate
rub

S

sack
sadness
safely
sank
Sat.
Saturday
save
saved
saw
scan
schedule
school
scold
Senate
senator
Sept.
September
shack
shear
sheep
shin
should
shrine
shrink
shrub
shrug
shy
shyness
sickness
signature
silver
sing
sink
skate
skin
sky
slay
sled
sleep

sleet
slight
slink
slip
sly
small
smear
smell
smock
snack
snake
snip
snub
sock
solve
soon
spell
spend
spent
spring
spy
St.
stack
state
stay
steep
stillness
straight
strap
stray
string
strip
summer
Sun.
Sunday
sway
sweep
sweet
swim
swing

T

tablet
taught
thank
thankful
then
thin
think
thought
Thurs.
Thursday
time
tired
too
track
tray
tries
trip
try
tub
Tues.
Tuesday

U

unclear
undo
unloved
unlucky
unsold
useful

W

wean
Wed.
Wednesday
weep
where
which
whine
why
wife

wing
wink
word
worst
would
wrap
wren
wring
write
wrote
wry

Y

year

Skill	Completion	Skill	Completion	Skill	Completion

Unit 1

Review Words .... ☐
Sight Words........................ ☐
Phonics: Syllables .... ☐
Phonics: Syllables and
    Schwa........................... ☐
Comprehension: Think
and Write........................... ☐
Comprehension Skills: Cause
    and Effect .... ☐
Writing Skills: Suffixes *-ly*
    and *-y*........................... ☐
Life Skills: Writing a Letter .... ☐
Unit 1 Review...................... ☐

Unit 2

Review Words .... ☐
Sight Words........................ ☐
Phonics: Consonant blend
    with *r* .... ☐
Phonics: *-y* and *-ink*......... ☐
Comprehension: Think and
    Write .... ☐
Comprehension Skills:
    Inference .... ☐
Writing Skills: Irregular
    Verbs .... ☐
Life Skills: Reading Coupons .... ☐
Unit 2 Review...................... ☐

Unit 3

Review Words .... ☐
Sight Words........................ ☐
Phonics: Consonant Blends
    with *s* .... ☐
Phonics: Long *-eet* and *-ean* .... ☐

Comprehension: Think and
    Write........................... ☐
Comprehension Skills: Stated
    Main Idea..................... ☐
Writing Skills: Prefixes *re-*
    and *un-* .... ☐
Life Skill: Reading a Report
    Card .... ☐
Unit 3 Review...................... ☐

Unit 4

Review Words .... ☐
Sight Words........................ ☐
Phonics: Consonant Blends
    with *l* .... ☐
Phonics: *-ock* and *-ate*..................... ☐
Comprehension: Think and Write ... ☐
Comprehension Skills:
    Implied Main Idea..................... ☐
Writing Skills: Adding *-ies*
    or *-s*........................... ☐
Life Skills: Reading a
    Prescription .... ☐
Unit 4 Review...................... ☐

Unit 5

Review Words .... ☐
Sight Words........................ ☐
Phonics: Consonant
    Digraphs..................... ☐
Phonics: *-ack* and *-ank*..................... ☐
Comprehension: Think and
    Write........................... ☐
Comprehension Skills:
    Sequence .... ☐

Writing Skills: Suffixes *-ful*
    and *-ness* .... ☐
Life Skills: Reading Park
    Rules .... ☐
Unit 5 Review...................... ☐

Unit 6

Review Words .... ☐
Sight Words........................ ☐
Phonics: Silent Letters..................... ☐
Phonics: *-ing* and *-ub* .... ☐
Comprehension: Think and
    Write........................... ☐
Comprehension Skills:
    Context .... ☐
Writing Skills: Abbreviations
    and Titles..................... ☐
Life Skills: Coping with
    Shyness .... ☐
Unit 6 Review...................... ☐

Unit 7

Review Words .... ☐
Sight Words........................ ☐
Phonics: *y* as a Vowel..................... ☐
Phonics: *-eep* and *-ear* .... ☐
Comprehension: Think and
    Write........................... ☐
Comprehension Skills:
    Drawing Conclusions..................... ☐
Writing Skills: Days and
    Months........................... ☐
Life Skills: Reading a
    Schedule .... ☐
Unit 7 Review...................... ☐
114–117 Final Review..................... ☐